HOW TO
GET INTO
LAW
SCHOOL

HOW TO GET INTO LAW SCHOOL

SUSAN ESTRICH

RIVERHEAD BOOKS

NEW YORK

RIVERHEAD BOOKS
Published by The Berkley Publishing Group
A division of Penguin Group (USA) Inc.
375 Hudson Street
New York, New York 10014

Copyright © 2004 by Susan Estrich

Book design by Stephanie Huntwork

Cover design by Walter Harper

First Riverhead trade paperback edition: September 2004

Library of Congress Cataloging-in-Publication Data

Estrich, Susan.
How to get into law school / Susan Estrich ; [introduction by Kathleen M. Sullivan].—1st Riverhead trade pbk. ed.
p.   cm.
Includes index.
ISBN 1-59448-035-4
1. Law schools—United States—Admission.   2. Law—Study and teaching—United States.   I. Title.

KF285.E878 2004
340'.071'173—dc22   2004053181

Printed in the United States of America
10   9   8   7   6   5

FOR MARC, WITH LOVE

ACKNOWLEDGMENTS

My thanks to my students at USC for their assistance, insight, support, humor, patience, and tolerance, not to mention fact-checking, chart-making, cite-checking, etc. Special thanks to my research assistants during this project, Christy Harper, Emily Brown, Ashley Nissenberg, and Matt Wickersham; to my administrative assistant, Danielle Ilan; to Dean Matt Spitzer and USC Law School for their support; to Amanda Urban and Susan Lehman for their wisdom and guidance; and to Isabel and James Kaplan, and Judy Estrich, for their love.

CONTENTS

BOOK TWO
WHAT YOU NEED TO LEARN

FOREWORD

My best friend Susan can teach anything to anyone. When I decided I wanted to be a law professor, my friend Susan took me over to her house and went to work on my presentation.

When she was done with the presentation, she went to work on the campaign. I ended up in the office next to hers at Harvard.

You could not be in better, kinder, smarter, wiser hands.

If anyone can teach you "how to" do it, she can.

If anyone can remind you why you once loved the law, and still might, she will.

KATHLEEN M. SULLIVAN

Dean and Richard E. Lang Professor of Law and
Stanley Morrison Professor of Law, Stanford Law School

HOW TO
GET INTO
LAW
SCHOOL

ARE YOU THINKING ABOUT LAW SCHOOL?

You've got company. As your aunt Bea will no doubt tell you, this is a terrible year. Well, it's always a terrible year, but in fact, more people signed up for the LSATs in 2003 than anytime in history—148,000, give or take, and nearly 100,000 people ended up applying. But so what. It's not like what "they're wearing," whoever "they" are. My senior year of college, three quarters of my classmates signed up for the LSATs. Pretty scary. But you can't let what other people are doing dictate your future. This is your career, your life, not your outfit for next season.

ARE YOU CRAZY?

I don't think so.

A lot of people will give you chapter and verse about miserable lawyers. I'll give it to you later myself. (See Chap-

LSAT AND ADMISSIONS TRENDS

YEAR	TOTAL TEST-TAKERS*	TOTAL APPLICANTS**	TOTAL ADMITTED**	LSAC MATRICULANTS**
1987–88	115,988	N/A	N/A	N/A
1988–89	137,088	N/A	N/A	N/A
1989–90	138,865	N/A	N/A	N/A
1990–91	152,685	N/A	N/A	N/A
1991–92	145,567	N/A	N/A	N/A
1992–93	140,054	N/A	N/A	N/A
1993–94	132,028	N/A	N/A	N/A
1994–95	128,553	84,300	52,200	42,200
1995–96	114,756	76,700	51,600	42,100
1996–97	105,315	72,300	50,400	41,600
1997–98	103,991	71,700	50,300	41,500
1998–99	104,236	74,400	51,300	42,200
1999–00	107,153	74,600***	50,300***	41,200***
2000–01	109,030	77,200	51,800	42,700
2001–02	134,251	90,900	56,500	46,000
2002–03	148,014	99,500	56,800	46,200

* Law School Admission Council, Test Administered Data, <http://www.lsac.org/LSAC.asp?url=lsac/tests-administered.asp>. Copyright © 2004 by Law School Admission Council, Inc.

** Law School Admission Council, Volume Summary Data, <http://www.lsac.org/LSAC.asp?url=lsac/LSAC-volume-summary.asp>. Copyright © 2004 by Law School Admission Council, Inc.

*** Due to changes in data collection methods, asterisked (*) data is not comparable to prior data.

ter 9.) It is an important topic. But I'm one who believes that the world actually needs great lawyers who understand the value of the rule of law. I want to help the people who care as passionately as I do about the law to get into the best law schools that they can and find their way as leaders in the profession, and in the world. I don't care whether you're liberal or conservative, Republican or Democrat, so long as you have a passion that brings you to law school and the drive to do something with your education.

Some years ago, when he was president of Harvard and I was a young professor there, Derek Bok, in his annual message, decried the brain drain into law. Why were all these smart kids going to law school?

His point was: there were so many more important things to do. Like science, and engineering, and mathematics. Why law?

Everybody hates lawyers until they need one. Then they only want the best. It says something important about our society that we do not ask a person to face the power of the state alone but guarantee him the assistance of a skilled advocate bound to act with the loyalty of a true friend. I define that as an honorable calling. We have a code of ethics that enforces it.

During the recent political season, I watched as operatives switched sides, trashing their candidates in the process. Lawyers don't do that. You'd get disbarred if you did. Call us what you will, it's against the Code. Greta van Susteren and I sat one night in New Hampshire and shook our heads in horror. "They talk about lawyers," she said to me. "We enforce standards of honor on ourselves." Imagine anyone else doing that.

It is vitally important that you understand why you're applying to law school, why you want to be a lawyer (or at least why you want a law degree and a legal education). But **don't apologize to anybody for your choice.** Unhappy lawyers should find better things to do. Most people who make lawyer jokes wish they'd gone to law school but didn't.

IS THIS REALLY
A "HOW-TO" BOOK?

Yes. (You don't have to apologize for asking, either. Getting into law school is serious business. Aunt Bea is certainly right about that.)

This is also a book for people who are about to start law school. And for people who are already in law school and are ready to look for their first job . . .

. . . And for people who are out there practicing law and can't remember why they went to law school in the first place.

WHAT DO I KNOW?

I am writing from inside the bubble.

Some of my best friends are the deans and admissions directors of the law schools that you want to get into. I know how their minds work. In some cases, I taught their minds to work. As my editor would say, I know all the inside stuff.

For instance, do you know how to get an interview at a school that doesn't give interviews? Do you know how to get the admissions director on the phone? Do you know how to set schools up against one another in a competition that could land you more scholarship money and a summer job, even if your parents are middle-class? Do you know which ratings system professors think is the best? Which local schools do better than national schools in getting their graduates jobs at top law firms? That kind of stuff.

Also, how *not* to blow an exam, piss off a professor, etc.

And, most important, what to do if your numbers aren't what you wanted, or if you hit the wall, or if you forget why you're in law school, or why you became a lawyer.

I'm not your typical "how-to" writer. Most of them are hired by one of the big outfits, the companies in the business of selling you programs, outlines, bar review courses, and everything else to prey on your insecurity. Their books are meant to look indistinguishable from the ones that they publish for business school students or would-be doctors. The more amusing books are written by recent graduates, still reeling from the experience, but they don't necessarily know much more than you do. They're fun to read, but you don't necessarily need more things to read, unless they are really very, very funny, much less books written by people who are still trying to figure it out themselves.

I'm the kind of person "how-to" books are trying to figure out . . .

WHY AM I WRITING THIS BOOK?

I've been teaching law for twenty-four years now, the first ten at Harvard and at USC ever since. I've also been teaching undergrads for the last decade, which has put me in the business of writing recommendations as well as receiving them. I've been at it long enough that one of my former students, Elliot

Spitzer, is now old enough to be the attorney general of New York.

I've been fascinated by admissions since I first started teaching at Harvard and used to sit around with Molly Geraghty, the director of admissions, trying to figure out what was happening to women applicants and students.

One of my sidelines, for my friends, has turned into helping their children do their applications. For obvious reasons, it is something parents can't do. I joke that I haven't been turned down since I applied to Radcliffe for myself, and it happens to be true.

What's also true is that I know what it's like to be rejected. I wanted to go to Radcliffe *so* badly I could taste it. It's thirty years, and then some, but I still remember the envelope. Very, very skinny. You know what that means: rejection.

That's really why I got so interested in admissions. I went to Wellesley because they gave me a big scholarship, and I studied like crazy for the LSATs. My numbers went way up from the SATs, but I was still insecure enough that I believed my sister when she said they got them backward on the card. I waited until Wellesley got their copy to breathe a sigh of relief. Picking Harvard Law School was easy.

My father started out at night school at Northeastern and then transferred to Boston University. He made *Law Review,* skipped classes, and went to the racetrack with his classmate Ed Brooke, who some years later was the first black to run for statewide office in Massachusetts. Ed was, and is, a Republican; I was a Brooke girl. He later became the first black to serve in the United States Senate since Reconstruction. I actually began my political career as a Massachusetts Republican.

My father practiced law in Lynn, Massachusetts, where I was born, a city north of Boston. He was the president of the bar and the Legal Aid Society. He prided himself on never sending a bill. All the time that I was growing up, we never paid for anything—everything was done by my father's clients. The linoleum-floor guy. The plumber. The car mechanic. The movers. All the afghans—from the wives. The cribbage boxes from the guys in prison, whom my father represented when other people wouldn't. Many people attended his funeral, and I had no money for law school.

My father loved his work. He was smart, and honest to a fault, and he understood how things were supposed to be. Law was the tool that gave him the power to make the system work; and he was respected for his ability to wield it.

On the day my father fell over with a heart attack, he was running to court on behalf of grandparents who were trying to hold on to custody of the baby who they were raising. He didn't even know the people; somebody had told them to call him. It was the kind of case that he would never expect to get paid for, but he had already won when he keeled over. He got a lot of satisfaction from winning. I wanted to do exactly the same thing on a much bigger scale.

I wanted power, too.

Not for its own sake, but for what I could do with it.

Now, maybe some would say I was wrong not to see that money is the only real power. But that's never been how I've seen it.

As a kid, I fell in love with all those political novels, and with watching political conventions on television. I dreamed of the day when I would be there myself (three years after I graduated from law school), when I would get to run a campaign (eleven years after I graduated). I dreamed of sitting around the Oval Office (fifteen years later), even of working there (never).

I tried practicing law with a firm, but I hated the billable-hours business, and not caring whether my client won or lost; I was a litigator doing endless cases where the motion practice contributed to settlement value and I couldn't make myself care enough or bill enough.

I did better writing appeals but I wasn't great at managing clients. I hated having to explain to them why we lost. I always regretted not being a prosecutor. I thought I would like that; I would care who won, but I would have had to give up politics at the time to do it. And I couldn't give up the politics.

What I knew for sure, from the days that I was in law school, was that what I would *never* do is teach. Those who can, do, I used to say; those who can't, teach. I'm not an intellectual, I would say, I'm a doer. But there came a time, when Reagan was president, and my party wasn't doing much in Washington, and there seemed no harm in giving it a try. And lo and behold, what did I discover? I loved it.

I ended up finding my passion in the classroom, and in a camera monitor doing television, and in my writing, and most of all, in students. I don't do my politics in the classroom. I have way too much respect for my students to do that. I teach in my classroom. I want my students to be their best, to remember their passions, and to fulfill them. The latest research confirms what I've known in my gut for the last two decades: that students come in as who they are, and if they're lucky, they remember who they are when they leave. My job is to give them the skills, give them the keys, to do something with it. That's what I try to do.

I feel like I got the keys to the Magic Kingdom in law school. I always will. I got respectability. To this day, there is a part of me that owes my self-esteem to that law school experience, and that sense of having triumphed in one of the last institutions proudly committed to merit above all else. It's sentimental, all those old rituals of the *Harvard Law Review*, with its file reviews and all-night meetings, but it touched me to the core, at a time in my life when I'd lost everything else I had. I sometimes wonder how it is connected, what is given and what is taken away, that I won the presidency of the *Law Review* at Harvard and then lost my father, that the other people at the funeral that day were all the members of the *Law Review*, dressed in interview clothes. Respect. We believed in that. Still do.

I believe in the law. Sounds corny, but it's true. I think of it as the glue that holds society together; what makes America work is that our civic religion is the rule of law.

As I look around the world today, it is so clear that some of the greatest problems we face are ones that can only be solved by the rule of law. We know how guns work and how missiles work, but we have barely a clue about how to get people of different religions and cultures to live together under the rule of law. Science is waiting for lawyers; generals are waiting for lawyers; ethicists are waiting for us.

I believe we need smart, decent, honorable people to be lawyers, to make the law, settle differences, keep people from turning disputes into wars; to assess damages, and force people to pay; to impose guilt, and punishment; to administer the rule of law.

I believe that thinking like a lawyer is a powerful discipline of the mind, training that will serve you well if you are pursuing a career in business or politics or the military.

I believe that being a lawyer gives you credibility in the worlds in which you travel, power to make change happen, the ability to do things that you haven't even thought of in various worlds where I haven't even been.

Think about what the American justice system accomplishes every day, albeit imperfectly, without anyone really noticing it or questioning it, until you try to duplicate law and order somewhere else, and begin to understand what it is that a legal system creates in a society.

So don't sell lawyers, or lawyering, or the rule of law short. It's tougher than science, done well, because you have to make it up each time, adapt democracy, re-create the rule of law, recognize that the underlying genius of the common law is that it looks easy and settled when it is anything but.

Sure, I'd love to sell lots of copies of this book. I've got my own kids' tuitions to pay. But I'd also like to see the best and the brightest of you go into law, succeed in law, find your passion in a career in this profession. I want to help you see your way through this process: by walking and talking you through, asking you the questions that you need to be asking me, and vice versa.

BUT ISN'T IT ALL JUST NUMBERS?

Who said that? Only if you let it be.

Don't get me wrong. You want to get the best numbers that you can. You have to get your head in that place. You have to understand what these numbers are about, how they are used, and why they become so important.

But are numbers all that matter? Not unless you give people *nothing else to judge you by.*

I think there ought to be a way, other than by your numbers, to convince people to accept you to law school; in fact, I know there is, because I've been helping kids for years; but the ratings games, and the fact that more and more schools and students buy in to it, has convinced too many of you that there isn't any other way, so you don't try hard enough and look hard enough. And it becomes another self-fulfilling prophecy.

Of course numbers matter from the schools' perspective. But there are other ways to identify great students and improve reputations than buying in to the system that values numbers above all, and that has schools throwing money and summer jobs at a few of the highly rated accepted students, and ignoring others whose need and potential may be greater. Admissions directors know this. They have many masters to serve. Give them something real and they will notice it.

One of admissions directors' pet peeves is the applicant who doesn't say anything . . . doesn't give them anything but numbers to consider.

I read these applications all the time. When they're done. A friend of a friend. I wince in pain, sometimes. The essays say absolutely, positively nothing. These are students who took the courses and bought the books and write these vanilla essays, and it turns out that they didn't study quite hard enough for the boards, and sometimes they didn't think quite creatively enough about where to apply, and by the time they come talk to me, it's a done deal, and it turns out it's a great kid who had a lot to say but was afraid to say it. They applied to all the top law schools, and then they didn't get in anywhere, and their hopes and dreams went up in smoke.

STOP.

Do not be defeated by the conventional wisdom before you begin. Applying to law school does not have to be an experience with an almost guaranteed unhappy ending. The conventional wisdom is wrong. It also leads nowhere.

WHAT IS WRONG WITH THE CONVENTIONAL WISDOM?

YOU DON'T HAVE TO GO TO A TOP LAW SCHOOL. Is it nice? Yes. Should you go to the best law school that you can? Maybe. It all depends on what you mean by best. Definitely don't do it "simply by the ratings." No sense to that. Far fewer schools are truly national than the number that claim to be.

You don't need to be convinced to go to a top law school. What makes them "top" is that most people don't get into them. If there are 14 top law schools, that means there are about 172 that aren't . . . so what kind of setup is that? Get serious. When was the last time someone over the age of thirty told you where they went to grad school?

What makes great lawyers is not always what makes great LSAT takers and great law students. Besides, Los Angeles is a more fun city than New Haven.

The point of going to law school is to become a lawyer, or at least to get a legal education, not to give your mother something to brag about at bridge club.

Many great lawyers have gone to law schools that the raters would tell you are not so great. You can get a very good education, and become an excellent lawyer, anyway. You can even become chief justice of the United States of America.

YOU DON'T EVEN HAVE TO WANT TO BE A LAWYER. Most people writing these books say you should only go to law school if you want to be a lawyer. That is very curious since most of them went to law school and aren't suc-

SUPREME COURT JUSTICES WHO ATTENDED SCHOOLS WITHOUT IVY WALLS	
SUPREME COURT JUSTICE	LAW SCHOOL ATTENDED
Chief Justice Warren Earl Burger	St. Paul College of Law (currently William Mitchell College of Law)
Hugo Lafayette Black	University of Alabama
Robert Houghwout Jackson	Albany Law School (only attended law school for one year)
Wiley Blount Rutledge	University of Colorado
Tom Campbell Clark	University of Texas
John Marshall Harlan	New York Law School
Charles Evans Whittaker	University of Kansas City
Thurgood Marshall	Howard University
Lewis F. Powell Jr.	Washington and Lee University

List compiled from information found at http://www.michaelariens.com/ConLaw/justices/list.htm

cessful lawyers themselves. If they were, they would have much better things to do than work for bar review companies writing these books. Some of them are businessmen who run their own test prep companies. They are also not lawyers. Or they are law professors, as I am, who have chosen not to be full-time lawyers. So who are we to tell you not to go to law school unless you're sure that you want to be a lawyer?

YOU DON'T HAVE TO KNOW WHAT SPECIALTY YOU'RE INTERESTED IN. I'm still deciding myself. Seriously, I will give you chapter and verse later, but the advice that this is something that you are supposed to know about the law or yourself is ludicrous.

WHAT YOU *DO* NEED TO KNOW

You don't need to know what job you want when you get out, but you need to know who you are, and what you care about, and what you're doing in law school.

You need to know these things about yourself or you'll have nothing to say in your application, nothing to hold on to when the pressures hit, nothing to fall back on when you're disappointed, and who knows what you'll turn into, much less what job you'll end up taking.

The less grounded you are in your own goals, the more vulnerable you are to everyone else's. The problem is not that you fail but that you succeed. You start desperately wanting to get into schools that you didn't know existed, hungering to work for law firms you've never heard of, looking down on the people you used to love. Or you just find yourself miserable and lost, with no idea what you're doing there, too tired to figure it out then. If you go to law school *not* knowing who you are or what you care about, you will end up a lawyer, and you may not be happy.

WHY ANOTHER BOOK?

Because there's too much bad advice out there. There are many people writing these books who say inexplicable things. I'll be reading along, and the authors will be explaining what's wrong with some of the popular ratings systems, and then all of a sudden they produce their own—and it's missing UCLA. Just missing. Nowhere in the top fifty. No explanation. Crazy. Why? Who knows why?

Then there's the book that's going along making sense until it advises you not to go to the University of Chicago Law School if you're interested in intellectual property. Not enough courses. A lot of people think it's the best law school in America! And you're supposed to be turning it down because you're counting courses, although in most cases, all you really should be looking at is size when you examine course offerings.

That book also tells you to think twice, or more, about doing *Law Review*, much less being president, because there are other "pleasures" in law school. (Like what??) This is not advice I would give. . . .

Because I'm not selling hats. Even the best books are trying to sell the rest of their courses. It has become an entire industry, and the conflicts among the various parts left me spinning. They could leave you broke. Hold on to your wallet. I spent a fortune just researching this book and I borrowed half the books I needed from the ever generous Bill Hoye, the much-quoted and wise dean of admissions at USC, who roped me into speaking to the Law School Admissions Council in Phoenix in June two years ago, when he was chairing the meeting, and reignited my interest in admissions. After reading the books, I expressed some horror at the emerging industry, and he pointed out that it was in fact no different ($7,500 for a competitive course) than what I was seeing at the secondary school level in our own city. Fair enough. It's still out of control.

Because I care. Passion, after all.

WHY ONE BOOK, ABOUT GETTING IN AND GOING, INSTEAD OF TWO SEPARATE ONES?

Because this way, you get to take a peek ahead . . . see what you're in for; see how it looks; see if it's for you. Because once you trust me, there's no telling what we can do and how far we can go together.

Because that's the secret: If you can find your passion, find something you care about, values to hold on to, the integrity at your core, that's what you really need to write a great application, push yourself to be your best, survive and succeed in law school itself, and find work that matters. That—not where you go, or what you get—is the "ball," as we like to say.

In writing a how-to book, my goal is not to help you somehow "pull the wool" over the eyes of Bill Hoye (USC) or Joyce Curll (Harvard) or any other admissions director.

No, my goal is exactly the opposite: **I want to help you get their attention.**

The last thing that you want to do is slip by. The goal is to stand out.

The students I want to help the most are the ones who have something to say and need help in finding their voice to say it. That's what this book is about. Because of one thing I am absolutely certain: Every single admissions director is listening and looking for students with passion and potential.

That's why they read every essay, every recommendation. Why we have people and not machines doing this job. They're looking for leaders.

If you have to make it up, it won't work. Work on it, yes. But no one can come up with it for you.

"What's *your* favorite book?" a candidate once barked at me, after I asked him the question, as if I could somehow give him the answer to the hated personal question. It doesn't work that way. It has to ring true.

I asked Bill Hoye, dean of admissions at USC, what keeps him going each year:

Every year, we'll take some "chances" by admitting a few applicants whose "numbers" don't compare at all favorably with the pool. Appli-

cants who clearly demonstrate that those numbers just don't do an adequate job of predicting their potential. What could be more rewarding than "taking a chance" (which probably is not a chance at all, but a sure bet) on an applicant who then goes on to do well academically and contributes in a very significant way to the life of the law school? These are the kinds of files that I look for. It is what keeps me going as I read seven thousand applications every year.

BOOK ONE
GETTING IN

{ 1 }

GETTING READY
What About College? Majors? Courses? Grades?
Recs? Graduate School? Extracurricular Activities?

WHAT TO DO IN COLLEGE TO MAXIMIZE YOUR CHANCES OF GETTING INTO LAW SCHOOL

Everyone knows the obvious: Get good grades. Fine. But the question is, in what? And what else?

WHAT SHOULD YOU MAJOR IN?

Pick a hard major. That's what they all say. "They" being all the admissions directors.

Pick an unusual major. Not pre-law or criminal justice. Science or math is great.

If you're interested in law, or trying to figure out if you are, why shouldn't you major in it? Two answers: 1) In many schools, those are considered "easy" majors. You never want to do anything that advertises you as a gut hunter. This is a very bad thing to be. 2) Law professors are snobs. They have far more respect for people who teach things that they don't teach themselves. (Note: there are important exceptions to this rule, as in Michael Sandel at Harvard, one of the most respected non-law-school law professors in the country, as there are to every rule, so don't insult your professor by saying you don't want a recommendation because law professors won't respect him; on the other hand, be careful before you write an essay saying you want to go to law school because of your constitutional law professor, whom no one on the Admissions Committee has ever even heard of . . .)

WHAT OTHER COURSES SHOULD YOU TAKE?

Consider philosophy, logic, math, or probability courses. These courses help on the LSAT, and will sharpen your analytical test-taking skills.

Don't forget the humanities. Do not forget things that will provide joy and relaxation later in life, when your days are filled with law. Art and music. Languages, absolutely. Learn yoga and meditation to deal with the stress you'll surely face.

Don't look like a gut hunter. Get good grades . . . if you've still got time. Push up that GPA. But not at the expense of "Cowboys and Indians," or "Politics and Television." Avoid courses that spell "gut." Every good admissions director will tell you that you're better off taking hard courses even if you don't do as well. Even better if you do well, of course. But look like a real student.

RELATIONSHIP OF UNDERGRADUATE MAJOR TO AVERAGE LSAT SCORE

MAJOR	AVG. SCORE	NO. OF STUDENTS
Physics/Math	157.6	689
Philosophy/Religion	156.0	1,884
Economics	155.3	2,916
Int'l Relations	155.1	1,546
Chemistry	154.5	893
Gov't/Service	154.4	812
Anthropology/Geography	154.1	898
History	154.0	5,819
English	153.7	6,324
Biology	153.6	1,858
Other Social Science	153.2	2,609
Engineering	152.7	2,656
Foreign Languages	152.5	2,002
Finance	152.2	2,009
Computer Science	152.2	468
Psychology	151.9	3,977
Accounting	151.8	2,340
Political Science	151.6	15,388
Communications/Arts	150.7	3,898
Marketing/Real Estate	150.0	1,826
Liberal Arts	149.8	1,148
Management	149.4	2,735
Sociology	149.3	3,129
Business Admin.	148.6	2,111
Health Profession	148.6	984
Education	148.2	823
No major given	147.6	5,289
Pre-law	147.3	1,076
Criminology	145.8	3,960

Michael Nieswiadomy, "LSAT Scores of Economics Majors," *Journal of Economic Education* (Fall 1998), available at www.uic.edu/cba/cba-debts/economics/undergrad/table.htm (based on 1994–95 test scores).

Learn to write. One of the most important skills not only for law school but also for many aspects of lawyering is writing clearly, quickly, and concisely. The problem for many law students is that they forget how to write when they're in law school, and

ADMISSIONS INDEX INFORMATION FOR THE ENTERING CLASS OF 2002

LAW SCHOOL	RANKING	X LSAT	X GPA	CONSTANT
Stanford University	Top 10	0.026	0.222	-1.96
Columbia University	Top 10	0.045	0.559	-5.512
UC Berkeley	Top 15	0.871	23.487	8.474
Boston College	Top 25	0.54	5.56	-42.64
Wake Forest	Top 40	0.508	5.601	0
University of Florida	Top 50	0.027	0.304	0.259
Arizona State University	Top 60	0.401	2.647	8.102
University of Houston	Top 80	1	10	17.2
University of Miami	Top 90	0.035	0.316	-3.533
Marquette University	Top 100	3.6	35.3	-26.1
Drake University	Tier Three	1	10	0
Howard University	Tier Three	0.356	3.198	18.542
University of Idaho	Tier Three	0.03	0.469	-3.493
West Virginia University	Tier Three	0.036	0.383	-4.195
California Western School of Law	Tier Four	0.433	2.65	6.643
Gonzaga University	Tier Four	1.273	10.139	-123.029
University of Dayton	Tier Four	0.035	0.32	-3.74
University of Tulsa	Tier Four	0.039	0.342	-4.158

KEY

X LSAT represents the number multiplied by the student's LSAT score

X GPA represents the number multiplied by the student's undergraduate GPA

CONSTANT represents the constant added to the result of the LSAT/GPA formula

Information found on the Pre-Law Advisors National Council Web site, available at www.planc.org/adminfo.pdf (January 2002); *see also* Timothy M. Hagle, *Law School Admission Index*, available at www.uiowa.edu/~030116/prelaw/lawschools00.htm (August 15, 2000).

then they have to learn it again when they go to law firms. But if you never knew in the first place, you haven't got a chance.

INDEX NUMBERS

Some schools rely on index numbers. An index number is a weighted average of your undergraduate GPA and your LSAT that takes account of how the individual school chooses to

GPA AT SELECTED LAW SCHOOLS: 25%–75%

School	2.8	2.9	3.0	3.1	3.2	3.3	3.4	3.5	3.6	3.7	3.8	3.9	4.0
Harvard University											▭		
Yale University												▭	
U. of Chicago								▭					
U. of California–Los Angeles									▭				
New York University									▭				
Georgetown University								▭					
U. of Michigan–Ann Arbor								▭					
Boston College					▭								
U. of Pennsylvania						▭							
U. of Connecticut				▭									
Tulane University			▭										
Pepperdine University			▭										
Wake Forest University		▭											
Loyola U. Chicago		▭											
Brooklyn Law School		▭											
Villanova University		▭											
U. of N. Carolina–Chapel Hill		▭											
Loyola U. (New Orleans)	▭												
U. of Detroit Mercy	▭												
Howard University	▭												

*See American Bar Association & Law School Admissions Council, *Official Guide to ABA-Approved Law Schools,* available at http://officialguide.lsac.org/search/cgi-bin/results.asp (2004) (Data is for the entering class of Fall 2002).

weigh those two factors as well as the "quality" of your undergraduate institution—which may be measured by the school's
past experience with students from your school.

This is the reason some colleges come to be seen as "feeder
schools" to certain law schools; they know what an A is worth,
and their graduates do well.

WHAT IF YOUR GPA IS ALREADY HOPELESSLY BELOW YOUR TARGET SCHOOL'S MEDIAN?

Create a trend starting now. It is essential to take measures to
think right now about what the story is going to be later. Do
everything you can to boost your grades. It is not too late.
Show them that you're a late bloomer. Show them that your
last three terms *are* in their range by *getting them there*. **There is
still time!**

MAJOR	NUMBER OF APPLICANTS	PERCENT ADMITTED	PERCENT ENROLLED
Physics	115	87.80%	60.90%
Biology, spec.	513	82.30%	66.30%
Environmental Sci.	456	82.20%	64.70%
History	5,178	78.90%	66.30%
Economics	2,610	78.10%	63.60%
English	5,017	77.00%	64.80%
Mathematics	328	76.50%	58.20%
Chemistry	453	75.70%	61.80%
General Biology	1,164	75.20%	61.70%
Psychology	3,828	73.20%	61.10%
Political Science	13,431	73.00%	62.50%

Carol A. Leach, *Undergraduate Majors of 1998 Applicants to U.S. Law Schools,* Chicago State University, available at www.csu.edu/PreLaw/lawmaj~2.htm (based on information obtained from
LSAC for the 1998 entering class) © by Chicago State University, 2003.

WHAT ABOUT RECOMMENDATIONS?

Know two professors well or your recommendations will be worthless. There are two kinds of recommendations: vanilla and valuable.

The majority are vanilla. "Mr. Smith was a student in my class. He got an A. He always showed up. His exam was great. So were his papers. He is very insightful. Well respected on campus. Active in community activities. From a fine family. Signed, Someone Important." Doesn't matter.

A valuable recommendation tells the person reading it something they don't know. It can generally only be written by someone who knows you.

It doesn't matter if they're famous. It matters if they know you well.

I remember the dean's-office people laughing at a handwritten recommendation letter from President Jimmy Carter that was mistakenly written to Dean Al Facks (it was supposed to be Al Sacks). Only when I wrote on behalf of the same applicant did it occur to them that it might be for real. It was, by the way. They'd taken it for a goof. Maybe a friend of his father. It wasn't. Goes to show . . .

Take a second or third course from the same professors. Go see them after class. I used to hate people like this when I was a student. Do it anyway. No "turkey bingo" (making fun of people who talk in class; you get cards, you see, and put their names on them in different order, and as they get called on, you cross them off, and at a certain point someone yells out . . .).

Get a job as a research assistant. It is a much better way to make the same wages as you do scooping mashed potatoes or stacking books. Some professors are quite nice people. They are extraordinarily smart, and capable of teaching you a great deal if you are willing to put up with them. Getting to work for some of them is actually a rare opportunity that many a grown-up would long for, but the vagaries of work-study grants are limited to arrogant undergraduate and graduate students.

Find a mentor. There's a difference between being respectful and learning and being a shameless suck-up. Shameless suck-ups know who they are, and nothing will stop them. If you're not one, you probably should be doing more of it.

CAN A PRE-LAW ADVISER REALLY HELP?

Some pre-law advisers give very bad advice. You need to take the measure of the pre-law adviser, find out if/how much the person is worth having as an advocate, and then approach/schmooze as necessary. Some of them maintain contact with lots of admissions deans and do more than push the paper around. Some don't. I've talked to lots of students about how much help they got from pre-law advisers. A very mixed bag. Most got none.

Be polite but ignore pre-law advisers who tell you that you don't need to study for the LSAT, that other students do just fine without taking the test prep, that you shouldn't spend your money or apply for a loan if you need one.

Adjust expectations accordingly. No need to ever offend anyone. The last thing you ever want is someone saying you're a jerk. But don't expect the pre-law adviser to get you into law school.

DO EXTRACURRICULAR ACTIVITIES MATTER?

No one seems to care unless you don't have them.

The Exception Is Community Service.

Don't even think of applying if you haven't done it. Especially if you're a rich kid. Don't quote me but it's true.

Everyone is looking for it.

Enough said?

And don't just tell me you went down to the soup kitchen every year and volunteered with your family. This is not enough.

WHAT ABOUT LEADERSHIP?

A number of admissions people told me that what made them different was that they were looking for leaders. No one told me they were looking for followers. Hear this, loud and clear: Every kid applying, in addition to having the numbers, did other things. This will not get you in. Its absence could knock you out.

AM I SAYING THAT JUST GOING TO SCHOOL FOR FOUR YEARS AND GETTING GOOD GRADES ISN'T ENOUGH?

Yes. That is exactly what I am saying. That is not enough. Big Brother? Big Sister? How about organizing a new chapter, or rescuing one? How about establishing a statewide program? Okay, citywide? The issue is not simply that you did it, but that you did it with intensity and commitment. That you were a leader. It's a measure of character. So is its absence.

The more privileged you are, the more it's expected. Unless you're an art major, I wouldn't make it the art-museum variety. I'd really look at the community you're in, and try to connect what you do to why you're pursuing a career as a lawyer.

By the way, it's also a great opportunity to figure out what you really care about, what your passions are, if you don't already know.

CAN A SO-SO STUDENT REDEEM HERSELF BY GOING TO GRADUATE SCHOOL?

NO. Okay, maybe. Do you have a master's in something? Did you get good grades there? **"In what, from where?"** is the best answer you get from admissions directors.

Remember, graduate school grades are *not* included in your GPA. But if you've got an MBA from Harvard or Wharton, the answer is it's going to help. If, on the other hand, you kicked around college for an extra couple years, and picked up a

> No one will read your thesis. Don't even send it.
> Admissions directors all hate getting these in the
> mail. Don't send videotapes or portfolios either.

master's, and never did anything much with it, and now you're
applying to law school, not only does it not get included for-
mally, but it might raise some questions about whether you
know what you're doing, and why.

WHAT ABOUT TRYING TO GET INTO
ANOTHER GRADUATE SCHOOL FIRST,
AND THEN THE LAW SCHOOL?

Watch out. This is a new one. There is no single answer to this
question. Just be careful. We're snobs. Most law schools, particularly if they're better than the other schools, operate inde-
pendently: We take whomever we want, and reject whomever
we want; we float on our bottoms, and we raise more money
than anybody but the business schools, so nobody gets to push
us around. Knowing that, don't expect any other graduate department (READ: public policy, criminal justice, communications, public administration, etc.) to be able to push a law
school into accepting you, and any suggestion to the contrary
is going to cost you a master's degree that will not in turn help
you become a lawyer if that's what you want to do.

{ 2 }

SHOULD YOU TAKE TIME
OFF BEFORE LAW SCHOOL?

That depends:

- Is it two years or ten years?
- Did you run the office or answer the phone?
- Teach skiing or run the ski school?
- Wait tables or start a restaurant?

"Don't tell me . . . you went to work as a paralegal because the name partner is a big alum of the law school and you thought that it would help you get in," one admissions director said to me.

Did I say, "Don't be a paralegal"? It's an old story. And then you never meet the big-name partner. Or if you do, it's hardly enough to get you more than a standard (useless) recommendation. Nor is two years as a paralegal, by the way, of any use whatsoever in getting you into law school; as to whether it helps you decide about going to law school, that depends: the danger is that it may convince you that you never want to be a lawyer because paralegal work can be so tedious and so awful and it's not what lawyers do. Go be something else, not a lesser version of what you will be.

DOES WORKING HELP GET YOU IN?

It might, if it gives you something to say. I talked to a great many people about this issue. The answer seems to be that many students aren't really ready for law school when they graduate from college, and that makes the process of applying very difficult. It's difficult because they really don't know if they want to go to law school, because they have no idea what they want to do, so they have nothing to say in the application, and they can be very unhappy when they get there. If you are one of those people, the point is not so much that you "need" to work in order to improve your chances, but that you will write a better application and present a stronger case when you are clearer yourself about what you're doing. And hopefully, your work, or time, or life experience will give you that insight.

Do you need the time, the experience, or the money? So, in addition to financial issues, the answer to whether people need time off before law school (and usually the answer is yes) is do you need time to figure out who you are, where you want to live, what kind of work you want to do . . . ?

Don't apologize if the answer is yes: for most young people, four years of college, their first four years away from home, will not be and should not be enough to figure this out. The other problem with going straight to law school, or almost straight, as

I did, even if you know who you are, is that I still haven't been to Italy.

WHAT SHOULD YOU DO?

Go to the Peace Corps, serve in the military, play professional ball, climb mountains, do campaigns, live abroad, travel, etc. Do you need time off to figure out where you're likely to be living, since the most important aspect of picking a law school, beyond the very top few, is location? Take it. Travel. See the country. Teaching school is one of the easiest ways to do it.

> *"When someone is ten years out of school, it is less and less meaningful to be looking at their GPA as a measure of their ability."*

All things being equal, having work experience is generally a plus. But not if it's just answering mail in a congressman's office before you apply to Georgetown. It's not that it hurts you, at least at first, but after a certain point, doing a certain kind of job starts raising questions about you that might not have been obvious in your college record. How long could you have been satisfied in that job? Why?

As you'll see later, certain kinds of jobs sell better on the road: Hollywood agents are better sold to Georgetown; former Capitol Hill staffers should think USC and UCLA.

One thing you will need from your work is a great recommendation; look around . . . who is going to write it? I am amazed by how many students never know the answer to that question. They never think about it while they are there. You must cultivate a mentor at work.

WHAT DO LAW SCHOOLS LOOK FOR IN PEOPLE WHO HAVE WORKED?

Obviously, there are basics: diligence, ethics, hard work, determination, and success. I remember being very relieved that I was fired from my job as the office manager of a vending company after, and not before, applying and being accepted at law school. In this sense, beware; even a terrible job can hurt you, if you are forced to explain why you were fired from it. For years, I had to explain why my jerk of a boss, a married man with children, fired me because his girlfriend lost her job and he figured that I didn't really need mine. Every single application or job clearance that I have ever filed includes that story.

More important, though, is **leadership.** What happened at the ski school? Did you change the way that they teach the kids? Then it works fine. If you waitress, organize a union, change the way they structure hours . . . make a difference.

I know what made my class at Harvard special. It was, first and foremost, the people in it. They were chosen for where they were going, and that is determined not only from the numbers, but from what you see in essays, activities, and work experience. You're looking for people who rise to the top in whatever situation they're put in, people who stand out, make change happen, make a difference. If they get fired, it's because they stood up. They are not followers. It sometimes creates friction during the three years. It is one of the things that makes good law schools seem like highly competitive places, even if individual students are eager to help one another. It creates challenges for professors and is one of the reasons that being a law professor has evolved into a job that requires that you be able to outwit even the smartest student—to make mincemeat of them sometimes—not so different from the way you train a puppy, or a cadet, although we profess not to do it anymore.

Does work experience increase your chances by 25 percent? I actually saw that on a Web site. The answer is of course not, although more and more law students are showing up with experience. Having something truly powerful or convincing to say on your application increases your chances by at least 25 percent above your numbers. Think of it that way. For many people, it takes work, literally, to provide that.

{ 3 }

ARE YOU COMMITTED?

"I decided I wanted to be a lawyer quite suddenly, in the middle of the first year in which I was taking nothing but math courses (I'd graduated from college and was on an NSF fellowship to work on my Ph.D. in math at Harvard), when it suddenly hit me that I couldn't imagine being happy spending the rest of my life communicating mostly with a blackboard rather than with Carolyn, whom I'd met a year earlier, and doing things almost nobody could understand, rather than using ideas to change people's lives, something that began to seem a lot more important to me at around the same time for the seemingly trivial reason that a pair of undergraduates whom I was coaching in intercollegiate debate got really screwed (in my opinion) because some debate judge voted against them and in favor of their opponents in the semifinal round of the national debate tournament, and did so (I thought) for basically bigoted and pig-headed reasons, which led me to think that becoming a lawyer would not only mean dealing with the ideas that lots of people care about and can understand but putting those ideas to work keeping

the good guys from getting shafted by the bad guys. It was as simple as that."

LAURENCE H. TRIBE
Carl M. Loeb University Professor
Harvard Law School

There's a story that we tell in politics about the chicken and the pig to demonstrate the difference between involvement and commitment. It's all about their role in a breakfast of bacon and eggs. The chicken, we say, was definitely involved. But the pig was committed.

You have to be committed to apply to law school these days. That didn't used to be true.

I did a little survey of some of my friends, including some of my famous ones. Michael Dukakis applied to exactly one law school, Harvard. So did Christopher Edley, the new dean of Berkeley. Both of them, by the way, are graduates of Swarthmore, and say they worked harder in college than in law school.

Both of them are also very smart, but if their kids or grandkids came to see me today, as they might at the right time, and were just as smart, I'd tell them that they would be out of their minds to apply to only one school, no matter who they are or how smart they are. It doesn't work that way anymore. There are no guarantees. I got into everyplace when I applied. I don't know anyone who does that anymore, even if they're much smarter than I. Honestly, I think the LSAT is harder these days; it certainly seems that way to me. More is expected in an application. There were no essays as far as Michael or Chris could remember; neither could even remember writing an essay. They just sent in a form. Got in. Sure thing.

Today it's a mystery. Kids come to me: How could I have

gotten into Yale and not Harvard? Makes no sense. Stanford, but not Yale. Sometimes. Very few get in everywhere. Certainly not at the top. UCLA, but not USC. Happens. Penn, but not USC. Ditto. Different schools have different strategies. No one talks about them. Or admits to them. Everybody needs insurance schools. So it goes.

There might have been a test prep service in my day but I can't remember. I wouldn't have had the money for it anyway. But the business was in its infancy. I studied by myself. Frankly, I was one of the few among my friends who did. But I'd been burned by the SATs, and I was determined. Now you'd be nuts, and I mean nuts, to go naked into the night with the LSATs. Ask any dean or law professor whether they'd send their own child to an LSAT prep course, or encourage them to save the money. I think I know the answer.

Applying to law school today requires commitment: time and money, the investment of the pig. Very few people really succeed in the effort without it.

The problem is, many people start out down the path in the mode of the chicken. Maybe you go to the pre-law meeting because you can't think of anything else to do, or because 9/11 made you feel vaguely public-servicey, or because the job market stinks right now. Or maybe you're one of those people who is a great test taker, and one of your parents is a lawyer, and you figure that they'll at least pay for law school.

Play a game with me:

Scott Peterson is on trial for his wife Laci's murder. You can be the prosecutor, the defense lawyer, or the judge; you can be the investigator or the jury consultant; you can be running the local newspaper; you can be Dan Abrams or Rikki Kleiman, commenting on the trial on television; you can even be the

Bad Reasons to Go to Law School

Your father did.
Your mother did.
Your brother did.
Your sister did.
You have nothing else to do.
You did well on the LSATs.
You're good at it.
You've already started.
It's a year shorter than medical school.
A lot of people are lawyers.

head of ABC News, whom I happened to clerk with. Or you can be reading the paper on the train on your way to some other job . . .

You can be Elliot Spitzer (my former student), the attorney general of New York, or you can be the lawyer for the indicted investors, or you can be the FBI guys who put the whole case together, or the federal prosecutors, or you can be writing about it all for the papers, or you can be bringing a class-action suit for small investors, or you can be getting ready to run for governor, or you can be practicing with a firm . . .

Or you can be tending bar in the Keys. Or teaching school in Harlem. Or running a little company, or acting, or writing, and figuring this out some other time.

Which is it? If you can't find a lawyer fantasy that excites you, there's likely to be a reason for that. Don't kid yourself. It's *your* life!

HOW HARD IS IT TO SAY NO?

To disappoint your mother/father/spouse/self is like breaking up. Thinking about it is always a lot harder than doing it.

If you can't bear to break your dying mother's heart, tell her you've decided to wait until (at least) next year when your chances for Harvard will be better (they will be, a year of experience, after all, can only enhance your application); you're already thinking like a lawyer, even if you don't want to be one.

But whatever you do, don't put yourself on a track that may carry you for the rest of your career to a place you know right now you don't want to be.

WHAT ELSE SHOULD YOU DO TO BE SURE?

Read.

Which ones can't you wait to read? Pick five to read right now. Or reread.

1. Gary Bellow and Martha Minow, *Law Stories* (1996). Gary Bellow was a wonderful man who taught public-interest law at Harvard with fervor and passion and was loved by generations of students and teachers; Martha Minow is just one of the most brilliant and wonderful people in legal teaching ever.

2. Gary Delsohn, *The Prosecutors* (2003). A top reporter spends a year as a fly on the wall in a really good prosecutor's office and writes about what he sees—better than fiction.

3. Alan Dershowitz, *The Best Defense* (1982). You love Alan or you hate him; I love him; he taught me to write appeals. I'm in the von Bulow case, paid for my first house, what a ride . . . Did he do it? Don't ask me . . .

4. Grant Gilmore, *The Death of Contract* (1974). On its face, it's a little book about contracts; really it's the answer to the common law . . .

5. John Grisham, *The Firm* (1991). Okay, the second-best legal thriller out there, by the most popular author . . .

6. Lani Guinier, *Becoming Gentlemen* (1997). The first African-American woman to be tenured at Harvard Law School—and it happened after I left, mind you—examines the experience of women in the classroom. I'll tell you, not all women agree; some think things are better; some don't . . .

7. Oliver Wendell Holmes, *The Common Law* (1881). I wouldn't dare try to summarize . . .

8. Judith Richards Hope, *Pinstripes & Pearls: The Women of the Harvard Law Class of '64 Who Forged an Old Girl Network and Paved the Way for Future Generations* (2003). A wonderful memoir by a brilliant woman who was out there before me breaking down the doors . . .

9. Richard Kluger, *Simple Justice* (1975). The story of *Brown* v. *Board of Education,* the case that changed America, holding separate but equal to be inherently unequal, the story of the people who lived it, the lawyers who argued it, of Thurgood

Marshall, who was the chief lawyer and went on to become the first black on the Supreme Court . . .

10. Harper Lee, *To Kill a Mockingbird* (1962). No synopsis required, reread it . . .

11. Anthony Lewis, *Gideon's Trumpet* (1964). The story of the case establishing the right to counsel for indigent defendants. Anthony Lewis ended up as the wonderful legal columnist for the *New York Times,* and is married to Margie Marshall, or rather Chief Justice Margaret Marshall of the Supreme Judicial Court of Massachusetts, best known for her courageous decision on gay marriage, forty years later . . .

12. Richard Posner, *Economic Analysis of the Law* (1971). The brilliant judge who in so many ways invented "law and economics," which has dominated academic thinking for much of the last three decades.

13. Jeff Toobin, *The Run of His Life* (1997). I may be prejudiced because he's my former student (I told you, I've been at it that long), but it's by far the best O. J. Simpson book in the batch.

14. Laurence Tribe, *American Constitutional Law* (1978). It's a treatise, but it's the best one ever written, and Larry is the guy who would've been on the Court in a different, un–Borked time; but having led the fight against Bork, he can't complain; he has led a principled life . . . And he's brilliant.

15. Scott Turow, *Presumed Innocent* (1987). By the author of *One-L,* and the best writer of legal fiction, if you ask me; what

better book to take on the plane, chill out with, just a great, great legal thriller; if it doesn't get your juices going . . .

16. Greta van Susteren, *My Turn at the Bully Pulpit* (2003). My friend and favorite television lawyer . . . more about Greta later; she is one classy, smart terrific woman . . .

Make your own list. The point of a reading list is to look for books that move you, for people who inspire you, for lives that thrill you. Or pay very close attention if none of them do.

The goal is not to fool other people into thinking that you want to be a lawyer, but to avoid fooling yourself.

{ 4 }

THE LSAT

"There are no problems, only opportunities."

—MOTTO OF MONDALE '84 CAMPAIGN

The LSAT is a giant-size opportunity. It is given four times a year. To sign up, go to www.lsac.org.

What Is the LSAT?*

The LSAT is a half-day standardized test required for admission to all 201 LSAC-member schools. It provides a standard measure of acquired reading and verbal reasoning skills that law schools can use as one of several factors in assessing applicants. The test consists of five thirty-five-minute sections of multiple-choice questions. Four of the five sections contribute to the test taker's score. These sections include one reading-comprehension section, one analytical-reasoning section, and two

logical-reasoning sections. A fifth section typically is used to pretest new test items and to pre-
equate new test forms. A thirty-minute writing
sample is administered at the end of the test. The
score scale for the LSAT is 120 to 180. The test is
designed to measure skills that are considered essential for success in law school.

*2004–2005 LSAT Regular Administration Dates***

Saturday, October 2, 2004

Saturday, December 4, 2004

Saturday, February 12, 2005

Monday, June 6, 2005

Saturday, October 1, 2005

Saturday, December 3, 2005

Saturday, February 4, 2006

* Law School Admission Council, *Frequently Asked Questions—
LSAT,* <http://www.lsac.org/LSAC.asp?url=/lsac/faqs-and-
support-lsat.asp>. Copyright © 2004 by Law School Admission
Council, Inc.
** Law School Admission Council, *About the LSAT,* <http://
www.lsac.org/LSAC.asp?url=lsac/about-the-lsat.asp>.

Where you will go to law school *may* **depend on your
score.** Your LSAT and your GPA determine your ballpark, the
arena within which you score.

For example, let's assume you're interested in Tulane. Your chances of getting in, speaking strictly numerically, can be found on the chart below. Many schools release similar information.

ADMISSION MATRIX FOR TULANE LAW SCHOOL PROBABILITY OF ADMISSION BASED ON LSAT & GPA

GPA/LSAT	120–144	145–149	150–154	155–159	160–164	165–169	170–174	175–180
>3.75	<30%	30%–49%	30–49%	75–90%	>90%	>90%	>90%	>90%
3.50–3.74	<30%	<30%	30–49%	50–74%	75–90%	75–90%	>90%	>90%
3.25–3.49	<30%	<30%	<30%	30–49%	75–90%	75–90%	>90%	>90%
3.00–3.24	<30%	<30%	<30%	<30%	75–90%	75–90%	75–90%	75–90%
2.75–2.99	<30%	<30%	<30%	<30%	50–74%	50–74%	50–74%	75–90%
2.50–2.74	<30%	<30%	<30%	<30%	30–49%	50–74%	30–49%	30–49%
2.25–2.49	<30%	<30%	<30%	<30%	<30%	<30%	<30%	<30%
2.00–2.24	<30%	<30%	<30%	<30%	<30%	<30%	<30%	<30%

Available at "http://www.law.tulane.edu/admissions/index.cfm?d=jd&main=matrix1.htm"

THE BOSTON COLLEGE ONLINE LAW SCHOOL LOCATOR MATRIX USING 25TH PERCENTILE LSAT AND GPA SCORES

	<145	145–149	150–154	155–159	160–165	>165
>3.60					B	A
3.40–3.60			F	E	D	C
3.20–3.39			I	H	G	
3.00–3.19		M	L	K	J	
2.80–2.99	Q	P	O	N		
<2.80	T	S	R			

SELECTION OF LAW SCHOOLS FOR SOME CATEGORIES
(LISTED BY THEIR 25TH PERCENTILE SCORES)

A) Harvard Law School Yale Law School Stanford Law School	K) Brooklyn Law School Wake Forest University Loyola Law School—Los Angeles
B) University of California Berkeley	L) Florida State University Indiana University, Indianapolis New York Law School
C) Columbia University University of Chicago	M) University of North Dakota University of Wyoming Syracuse University
D) Cornell University University of California, Los Angeles University of Virginia	N) Willamette University Samford University, Cumberland University of Akron
E) University of Colorado	O) Albany Law School University of Detroit Mercy Howard University School of Law
F) Drake University	P) North Carolina Central University
G) University of Texas Boston College Law School University of Pennsylvania	Q) John Marshall Law School
H) University of North Carolina Ohio State University University of California, Hastings	R) University of South Dakota Western New England College
I) Baylor Law School University of South Carolina University of Houston	S) Oklahoma City University Appalachian School of Law
J) Boston University	

Data from the Midwest Association of PreLaw Advisors *Law School Admissions Profiles, Fall Entering Class 2002–2003*. Supplemented with *The Official Guide to US Law Schools*, 2004 Edition. Developed by Dom DeLeo & compiled by J. Joseph Burns. Available at http://www.bc.edu/offices/careers/gradschool/law/lawlocator/match.

Ten points in Boston is the difference between Northeastern and Harvard.

Ten points in New York is the difference between Brooklyn and Columbia.

Ten points in Los Angeles is the difference between UCLA and Southwestern.

Are you focused yet?

"How did you get into Harvard Law School?" I asked Bert Fields, one of Hollywood's best-known—and best—lawyers and an undergraduate at UCLA. He replied, "By getting the best law boards in the state of California." Only that.

Sad truth: Studying more will not guarantee you better numbers than someone else who doesn't study as much. But it will get you better numbers than YOU would have gotten without studying. And that's the point: **To do your absolute best.**

The more committed that you are, the better you will do. The LSAT does not test prior knowledge. All it tests is reading and thinking and preparation. That means preparation is of the essence. Not everyone has the capacity to score a 180. But almost everybody can improve her score through intense preparation. The more you prepare, and the more you respect the process, the better you will do.

Think of the LSAT not as a burden but as a chance to get ahead by being more committed than other people.

Should you take a course? Yes.

Should you hire a tutor? Yes.

How much should you study? More than you ever dreamed of.

What should you do? Become a nerd.

Is three weeks enough? No.

Understand that you are learning a foreign language.

Do not try to be too smart. Respect its rules. Come up with a system and stick with it. Eliminating wrong answers tends to be as important as identifying right ones.

WHAT ABOUT COURSES?

The conventional wisdom is convenient, but wrong. The conventional wisdom is that the courses really don't help that much, substantively anyway. That with a little determination, you can easily do at home what other people are spending $1,000 and more and paying for private tutors to do.

Notice how convenient this is. If it's true, then wealth doesn't matter so much, and we, the law schools, shouldn't feel guilty about continuing to rely on such a convenient measure of ability.

But is it true? In the aggregate? Does it make any sense at all?

If it could be easily done at home, why would people line up to pay? I did it at home, in the days when courses weren't quite as common, and it was incredibly difficult, and I'm as disciplined as can be.

INTENSE PREPARATION IS WHAT MATTERS.

Every waking minute you have. Every dime you have. Get a tutor if you can't stay awake for the class. You'll hate it. It's no fun at all.

Most people don't engage in intense preparation. They study an hour or two a day. NOT ENOUGH. This is your future. They take a course, like going to the gym, expecting it to do the work for them. "Are you studying for the LSAT?" I ask them. "Oh yes," they say. What does that mean? It means they're taking a course. Maybe a machine will do the sit-ups. "How'd you do," I ask them. "Not as well as I'd hoped," those people always say.

> *Not doing the homework is like watching an exercise class.*

DO ALL OF THE HOMEWORK.

All of it. It is a waste of time otherwise. I promise. Who's cheating whom? Ingest. This is it. Remember: The best way to make the case that your grades do not reflect your ability is to get a much higher LSAT score. The best way to get into a bet-

ter law school than the college you attended is to get a high
LSAT score.

> **UNFAIR BUT TRUE:** Because of the way rat-
> ings are done for law schools, high LSATs and a
> good essay explaining away your lousy grades will
> not get you into every top school, but they will
> get you into a few who are determined to in-
> crease their ratings since high LSATs *or* high
> GPAs increase ratings, so there are schools that are
> happy to take students with one *or* the other . . .

If you can't afford to take a course, create one. Do what
law students do. Form a study group. You are not competing
against your five friends. Advertise. Make it a larger group.
Make it a singles group. Make it anything that will meet every
day at a church/synagogue/whatever. In advance of the group,
each person should have spent three hours answering the same
sample exam. At the study session, you should go over the
exam, going around the table and simply explaining, at random, why each answer is correct. At random. Just do it. Hire a
law student to supervise the group.

RESPECT WHAT YOU'RE LEARNING.

Don't try to understand it; learn it the way you would a new
language, complete with its own set of rules of grammar, logic,
sentence structure, and the like. You are not smarter than it. It is

smarter than you. In the short time that you have to learn it, your job is not to change it but to figure it out.

There is nothing inherently logical or intuitive about the LSATs. It is not a test of native intelligence. Or ability. Or law. Or anything else, necessarily, except it.

Case in point: Me. I took a sample test. A few weeks ago. Sailing along just fine. Until I got one wrong. Why? I knew it was wrong the minute I marked the answer. I went back. "I bet they wanted this one," I thought. But I wouldn't want this one. It wasn't a very good answer. It was a lousy correct answer, I thought to myself. I started to get annoyed. A really lousy answer. I remembered everything I hated about law boards. It's a different language. No smart-alecks here. Learn their language.

If I couldn't ace it without learning the language again, without studying, do you think you can???? Sorry, but I'm pulling rank to make a point. It takes time and practice to learn a new language no matter how smart you are. It takes respect and recognition that that's what you're doing. It takes a fundamental attitude of deference going in, that too many would-be law students lack, and by the time they get that they're missing it, it's way too late.

Be careful when listening to what other students say. The students who do best in LSAT prep classes are the ones who understand that they are learning a board game. The ones who don't get it think it is their job to prove that the right answer is wrong.

WHAT IF YOU'RE HAVING TROUBLE STUDYING?

Do It Backward

If you're having trouble, **start with the answers.** That way you won't get angry with the test writers. You want to figure out why the right answer is right.

Nearly thirty years later, I can still remember studying for law boards this way. Yours is not to reason why at this point but to understand. It's *Jeopardy!* and you want to win. The way you psyche out a system is by figuring out how the system works. So look at sample tests and work backward from the answers, when you're having trouble.

Familiarity

Get every practice test that you can. Do each one. Go over it. It doesn't matter if you disagree, as long as you remember to mark their answer as correct.

Eliminate, Then Guess

Most multiple-choice exams, beginning with this one, turn more on reading comprehension than anything else. It's all there: if you can focus, eliminate, and keep your eye on the ball.

Your first instinct in taking a test is always to look for the right answer. What we (my students and I) found in taking the law boards (again) was that most of the time you had to find the wrong answers; most of the time you're going to get very frustrated looking for right answers and have a much better chance eliminating wrong answers.

The minute you see something in an answer that's wrong, eliminate it. In most cases, there is no choice but to eliminate all the wrong answers and then choose the one that isn't wrong.

It is very hard to write a multiple-choice test. To make a wrong answer both plausible and wrong, you make it sound right and then throw something wrong in it. Look for the wrong word, for a concept that is all of a sudden out of place, for "just a tiny something out of place" in what is otherwise the best answer. It's wrong. If an answer looks great except for one little thing, it's WRONG. The one that doesn't have anything WRONG in it is RIGHT. It's not the best answer you're looking for, but the RIGHT answer, that is, the NOT WRONG answer.

Eliminate the ones that you know are wrong, then guess among the remainders. Better than blind guessing. Never leave anything blank. Keep moving. If it's too hard, come back later—they like to mess people up by having five (a)'s in a row . . . don't worry about that.

When you're guessing:
- **First,** go with your instinct.
- **Second,** if you have no instinct, go with the letter you've used least.
- **Third,** once you've picked a letter to guess, always guess it.
- **Fourth,** if you really want to get scientific about guessing, powerscore.com analyzes slight variations in which letters get used . . . way beyond me, I should add.

Remember that you don't have to get 100 percent. You do have to not get bogged down. Know how long you can spend on a question. Save the hardest stuff in each section for last. Don't panic if a question is impossible. Just skip fast and keep going. Make your best guess and keep moving. Eliminate and go. Go and eliminate. Like life.

Opinions can't be right or wrong. Therefore, they usually can't be the right answer. In many cases, an opinion thrown into an otherwise right answer may be the red herring you're looking for to eliminate an answer.

If it's too fancy, it's wrong. If it requires too much thought, if you're the only one who could know it, if it's not capable of being known from what's there, it's WRONG.

> **Story to remember:** D.C. bar, summer 1979, I am working for Justice Stevens. A case had been argued that term where the court was equally divided on the question of criminal procedure. Justice Powell had recused himself, but he would be sitting in a similar case next year; and, lo and behold, I go to take the bar that morning, at the end of my clerkship year, and there is a hypo involving precisely that situation.
>
> I go back to chambers, and chew it over with Justice Stevens; we discuss how we think Justice Powell will vote; after a good twenty minutes of this, we finally remind ourselves that if we aren't sure, the person who wrote the bar exam probably has no idea. I made the question too hard. The answer had to be something simple . . .

Don't be too smart for your own good. Remember: reading comprehension is what the whole exam is testing, not what you learned in tenth grade.

Keep It Simple, Stupid . . . and you'll go a long way in the law.

TIMING IS EVERYTHING. IT DOESN'T MATTER HOW SMART YOU ARE IF YOU DON'T FINISH THE TEST.

Given enough time, you could probably answer every question right. But you don't have unlimited time. That's the rub. The game is to get as many right as you can in the little time that they give. You have to know how quickly you have to get through each section, how to use every second well, how to move without stopping. You should have your own minisystems in place for reading comprehension, analytical reasoning, even for guessing, so that you spend every second thinking, not doing anything you could have prepared for in advance.

For analytical reasoning, for instance, you know that you have to draw it. You don't even have to know what the questions are to know that you have to draw it. So start drawing. Practice it. Get to the point where you can draw as you read. Where you can't read without drawing. It's the only way you'll finish.

Know your symbols. Have your own.

For reading comprehension: You're going to need facts. Numbers. And a point of view. Circle them as you go along. Things that are "right" and "wrong." Skim the questions before you read. Read the ones you're interested in first. Save the one that you hate for last. Remember to *never* use information that you learned in eighth grade. *It has to be in the selection.*

Know how long you're allowed to spend on a question before you have to move on.

Don't Forget the Writing Sample

To be honest, I've never read one in my life. But a number of faculty members have told me that in close cases, they consider them decisive. I can't tell you how much sense that makes to me. In a world in which you can hire someone to do almost everything else for you, I can see why people will in-creasingly start looking at that as an honest tie-breaker in close cases.

KEEP A STUDY JOURNAL.

It is the only way you will be honest with yourself about how much you study. Write it down every day. How many hours did you study? How many tests did you do? Does this sound familiar, dieters? It should. We all know if you don't write it down, you lie.

HOW IMPORTANT IS IT TO YOU?

If you're not willing to put in the time, it is absolutely worth asking yourself why you're doing this in the first place. I prom-ise you that you are setting yourself up: the only people who look back with regret are those who start off believing they could/should have done better, and didn't, and therefore sold themselves short . . .

I know many people who told me that truly intense prep-aration raised their scores ten points. Ten points is a world of difference. Nothing against Cardozo, but it's not NYU; noth-ing against Pepperdine, but it's not USC . . .

Three months is nothing in the grand scheme of things.

I am not a snob, but if you have the capacity to do well, why not do it the first time, and spare yourself and everybody else a whole lot of trouble? Why look back with regret? Why wonder?

WHAT ABOUT TEST DAY?

Get there early.

Go in and do your best. If you've studied, rehearsed getting to the test site, eaten your usual breakfast, set two alarms, done your practice tests, you're totally prepared for everything. You know how to budget your time, guess, not waste time reading directions . . .

AND AFTERWARD?

You know that the *only* ones you will ever remember afterward are the ones you got wrong.

You know to never, ever, ever discuss specific questions afterward with anyone no matter how great the temptation.

You know to forget everything you possibly can about the test the minute you walk out.

You know that the more you think about the individual questions afterward, the more bad luck you bring on yourself.

You know that thinking about how well you did makes you do more poorly; you will be punished for negative thinking, so you should just forget about it, and think about your applications instead.

Keep your perspective. Where did Johnnie Cochran go to law school? Don't know. How about Rudy Guiliani? Bernie Kerik?

Sure it would be great to go to a "top" law school. You don't need me to tell you this. You don't need a book to tell you this. Most law schools aren't "top" or there wouldn't be a top.

But it's whether to be a lawyer, not where you start to become one, that's the key question.

After your first job, it's where you work and what you do that counts. Say that over and over again as you prepare to look at your score.

Mark Geragos went to Loyola Law School. Mario Cuomo went to St. John's University Law School. Chief Justice Warren Burger went to St. Paul College of Law. The LSAT does not predict who can convince a jury, close a deal, make a judgment call.

AND THE NUMBER IS...

There are two possibilities when you see the number. Let's deal with the good news first.

Good News

Okay. Skip this if you didn't get what you want. My life has been full of bad news and good news. I'm a single mother who pays two mortgages. You don't have to be jealous of me. If you get a great number, don't stop reading. Things don't necessarily go swimmingly from here. You still have to be the master/mistress of your own fate. Is it possible that even with a great number, things could go wrong? Yes, it happens. But not to you if you're smart. How do you make sure? By writing a great essay. By getting great recommendations. You are in a position to get a great deal—potentially, to get a merit scholarship, get your ticket punched, get your way paid, a summer job guaranteed, which turns into a permanent offer, which turns into more money than I make, or maybe a clerkship someday. Surprised? Didn't know that? To be honest, I didn't know either, until I started researching this book—that's how much things have changed since the days when I was the first law school graduate to work after the third year. So curse the sunshine, or collect. Here's what I recommend. If you get a great score: Congratulations. Apply to the top schools. But don't be too cocky. Put together a fabulous package. Make the best application you can. Now is not the time to start being lazy. No, you cannot go to the movies now. You have to work on your essay, focus on your recommendations, figure out what you're doing here. Then, once you get admitted, pick the three or four places where you want to go, and go to their admitted students days and start cultivating the admissions deans, let them know what it would take to get you, establish "relationships," decide where you really want to be, play them against one another, and you can laugh all the way to the bank. But right now, there's still work to be done.

That's for the lucky people.

I have always wanted to go through life as one of the lucky people, trying to capitalize on life's advantages. If you are one of those people, at least have the grace and the courtesy and the good manners not to flaunt it, okay? It is hard to be on the other side of the looking glass, looking in. Even if it always turns out that what you see, looking in, is never as good as what you imagine must be there when your nose is pressed against that window, assuming all those people must somehow be better/smarter/cleverer/more insightful/more disciplined/ more something than you are. What if they're not better at all? What if the emperor has no clothes? What if we knew that all along? Which, of course, we did . . . So why were we so afraid to tell anyone? As my son would say, did we think they would be mad at us? Probably.

Not As Good News

So you didn't get a 179. Or even a 169. Or even a 159. Disappointed? You're not the only one. Almost every student I've ever talked to about LSATs has told me that they expected to get the best score that they ever got in a practice test and are crushed, and, of course, furious at the testing company, when their score falls somewhere in the midrange.

Okay, so maybe they should've studied a little harder, but maybe you studied as hard as you could, and that's just what it is. Which is it? When they're disappointed with their scores, what everyone always wants to know is:

Should You Take It Again?

• Only if something went wrong.

• Only if there's a real reason to think that you'll do substantially better the second time.

• Two similar scores actually raise questions about your judgment.

• More than two and I really start to wonder.

If in twenty practice tests, you've only broken 160 once, and have hovered at 155, I know what I'm betting on and it's not schools whose median is 164.

Now, if you've hovered in the mid–160s, and only dropped below 160 once, and come test day, you're sick as a dog, or fought with your girlfriend the night before, or freak at the test, and get a 155, I'd tell you, by all means, take it again, explain to the schools what happened, turn it into a story, and you'll probably get your 164 the next time, and be fine—I know a number of students who did.

But if you've tested in the 155 range and studied like crazy, and it's a 155 you've got, then you need to accept your number. That doesn't mean giving up on a dream school if its range includes 155. The challenge is to put together the strongest application possible, so that if X school is going to take someone like you with a 155, it will be you.

{ 5 }

MAKING THE CASE
FOR YOURSELF

What Makes You Sparkle?

WHAT DO LAW SCHOOLS
REALLY WANT TO KNOW
ABOUT YOU?

No, not who your father is. Too many people labor under
that misunderstanding. Frankly, we don't care. Almost no one
has a father who is important enough for law schools to care
about. Important fathers are a pain in the you-know-where.

Sure, we want you to grow up and be rich, successful,
and generous. Everyone wants alumni who will turn out to
be the most generous and successful. But that's down the
road. Short run, we don't like dropouts. We expect everyone
to come and stay for three years. We budget that way. NO
room for mistakes. So the essential questions are pretty pedes-
trian ones:

1. **Can you do the work?** Do you have the ability?
2. **Will you do the work?** Do you have the commitment?

Can you and will you? If admissions people make mistakes, deans and people like me—professors—will not be happy. It is no fun to have students who really can't get it, or to have dropouts in the middle of the year, because you can't fill those spots in the second semester. If there's any question about your ability or your commitment, you have to answer it before anything else can be addressed. If there's any doubt, you're out. It is a measure of how rarely admissions directors fail that way upward of 90 percent of the people who enter most law schools graduate three years later.

Only if the answer to the first two questions is yes, do you even get to the third question.

3. **What else do you bring to the table?** Where's your "sparkle"? as my friend Molly Geraghty at Harvard used to put it. What makes you different from the hundreds, if not thousands, of other people with the same numbers you have? The goal of an admissions director is to put together a group, a family (as more than one described it), or a community. What unique contribution can you make to that community?

WHY DO NUMBERS COUNT SO MUCH?

Because they are the easiest way to answer the first two questions.

An LSAT score in the ballpark says you *can* do the work. I know about the literature establishing that the LSAT is biased against minorities and women; indeed, there were briefs so arguing in the Supreme Court affirmative-action cases. You can write me a paper on it if you take one of my classes. But first you have to get in. And the LSAT does correlate with first-year grades and bar passage. The other thing that LSATs do is influence the law school's own ratings, which influence what the alumni think, what the provost thinks, what the faculty think, how the dean is thought of, etc. Now, I can also show you extensive literature that proves that the law school ratings are bogus, biased, BS, etc. But do deans live or die by them? Yup.

A GPA in the ballpark says you *will* do the work. When we see someone with a high LSAT and low GPA, my admissions gurus explained, we know we have a student who can do the work, but it's a question of whether he will; the low grade point tells you that this is a kid who doesn't try and doesn't work hard. He's got the ability, but he just doesn't do it. The question is: Why not?

That's a question that this student will have to answer in the rest of his application package. If he doesn't, then he won't get in.

> If there is any question about your ability to do the work or your commitment to do the work, then you have to answer it in your file. Your application is your opportunity to make the case for yourself. For what you have to offer the school.
>
> Think of the rest of your application as a package **designed to answer the questions that the law school has about you, and to persuade them that your value is greater than your numbers.**

It includes:

• A great **Personal Statement** that the people who read will remember for more than thirty seconds and that convinces deans/professors that you really have something to add to the school.

• Great **Recommendations** from people who can describe you as a real person and who actually know you, your work, and your potential.

• Notes from the **Personal Interview** from your visit to your first-choice law school(s), as well as from the receptionists and secretaries who were so impressed by your courtesy and pleasantness when they dealt with you.

Potentially:

• A **Flag** that's the result of the inquiry from the impressed faculty member whose class you visited.

• A **Personal Note** from your pre-law adviser to the dean of admissions telling her that "this one" is really special and that X school really is your first choice.

It's one sparkling file, wouldn't you say?

It is a lot of work. It probably makes you tired just to think about it. But what the heck. It's just your future. **Apply early. It only gets harder.**

{ 6 }

THE PERSONAL
STATEMENT

*"As best as I can remember, none of the schools to which I applied
(Harvard, Yale, Michigan, Chicago, and Northwestern) required
application essays in 1945."*

—JUSTICE JOHN PAUL STEVENS,
U.S. SUPREME COURT

Things have changed! This is what Collins Byrd of the University of Minnesota says about the personal statement:

The second most important part of the application is the personal statement, or essay. (The most important pieces are the LSAT and undergraduate GPA together.) The personal statement is the vehicle with which Jane Average can really set herself apart. It is the one place where an applicant can tell the admissions committee what the applicant really wants the committee to know about her. The personal statement is the tool to tell us about the badges of courage that each person carries, in addition to interpersonal skills, work experience, activities outside of work or school, career focus, motivation, the ability to empathize, and problem-solving skills.

People really need to write a good personal statement. The LSAT and GPA tell me, in some way, shape, or form, what an applicant has achieved over time. The personal statement, though, allows the applicant to tell me what she has had to go through to achieve those things.

Things that never work:

• *Videotapes or cassettes that are sent in for additional support to an application. I don't have the machines in my office or the time to look or listen to such material. Besides, lawyers, not videotapes and cassettes, represent people in criminal cases and legal issues. Don't forget that the practice of law is a human endeavor. Don't dehumanize it any more than it already might be by sending us cassette recordings.*

• *Portfolios from professional models. Never, never, never do anything that takes attention away from the knowledge and wisdom that is located in your brain. Photographic portfolios do just that; they take away attention from your brain. On the other hand, if you have little to nothing in your brain, and the portfolio is your major ticket to success, then you are on your own.*

• *Creative writing and use of humor. Be careful. What you write or say may be high on the creativity scale and low (sometimes very low) on the impact scale.*

WHAT IS THE PURPOSE OF THE PERSONAL STATEMENT?

1. To answer any open questions about your ability and commitment.

If there are questions about your grades, what are the answers?

Is there a trend? Did you do better in your major?

2. To provide the school with additional information about who you are and the obstacles you have overcome to achieve what you have.

Were you raising your younger siblings, fighting illness, playing football, working full-time, getting divorced, etc.?

Are you half Korean and half African-American? You don't have to repeat what's in other parts of the résumé, but you can't expect a school to be a mind reader. If you want to be considered according to the affirmative-action standards approved by the Supreme Court in the Michigan case (this is a "how-to" book, remember, not the place to debate the standards), you have to make sure they know who you are. TELL THEM.

3. To demonstrate your character, passion, ambition, and drive to convince them that you will add more to the class and do more with the education that they are offering than the other people just like you in that pile of theirs.

> This is where you can make a difference right now. But it has to ring true. It has to sing. It has to be written as well as you possibly can write it. It has to be tailored to the school.

Look at the number of people who apply to your first-choice school. The director of admissions reads that many personal statements. He or she looks at every file. What will make him remember yours? What makes yours different from every other one? Imagine that he gets to yours late at night, when he's tired and about to call it a night. He reads the first few sentences. Will he remember them in half an hour? Would anyone? If the answer is no, start again.

It does not matter if you have lived a boring life. It does not matter if nothing has ever happened to you.

HOW DO YOU WRITE YOUR BEST PERSONAL STATEMENT?

Write about you, not about law. The books that tell you to focus on what specialty you want to practice and write essays about it are just plain silly. Don't try to be too substantive or you run the risk of, yes, sounding stupid. Whoever is reading your essay knows the stuff better than you. They also know your numbers, and all that. They know your résumé. They know why the world needs more lawyers.

Most young people haven't got a clue. Every day, I meet young people from incredibly interesting and powerful families who tell me that they've written essays about their views on international law. Asleep, I know more about international law than they do. And it's not even my area. So does whoever will read their applications. On the other hand, I have no clue how growing up in their various families shaped them, or what they see as their futures. If they look like leaders of the next generation, any school would want them. If that doesn't occur to them and if it's a vanilla essay with recommendations from fancy people, then rejecting them simply lets admissions deans make the point that just because somebody has a fancy name doesn't mean they automatically get in.

Remember what you're trying to accomplish. It doesn't matter what the story is, or what it's about. It doesn't matter if "nothing" has ever happened to you in your life. It could be something that happened in a chance encounter, in a moment at work, in a second . . . The point is what it tells us—the reader—about you, about who you are, what kind of person you are, what your potential is . . .

You're looking for a story because a story is the easiest way to communicate that—not because anyone cares in particular what it is that happened. Think of the trait of yours that you are trying to communicate—what is your strongest attribute, your strength, the source of your drive, the fire that burns inside you, and what will make you take the same legal education that the next guy or girl is getting and do more with it?

What makes you different? What will you contribute here? Some people pick a particular moment, a particular decision, or a dramatic instance that summarizes who they are. You can use all kinds of tools. Who will you be in ten years? Think about movies, stories, pictures . . . Give me a scene in your life. Draw it sharply. Grab me. What was the worst moment in your life? The worst thing that ever happened to you. If it looks like you've lived on easy street, and you haven't—TELL ME. Show humility.

Where does your ambition come from? Be proud of it. Have you noticed that articles in magazines or newspapers often begin with an anecdote? Instead of writing about a program you participated in, write about a child whom you helped.

Write about an issue that you care about and feel passionately about. The point is to demonstrate your passion, the power of your advocacy, your commitment. Imagine that you're Andy Cornblatt at Georgetown reading eight thousand of these a year, or my friend Joyce Curll, who is looking for people who will be up to the challenge of Harvard Law School.

You can't decide on the day that you apply to law school

Interview with Ann Coulter

Do you remember what you wrote your application essay about?

Yes! I wrote about affirmative action. My first point was that the theory of "diversity" assumed that a person's race was a proxy for beliefs, viewpoint, ideas, life experience, etc. etc., which was a strikingly racist assumption. Moreover, what was beguiling about "diversity" at a university was the diversity of ideas, not diversity of superficial physical characteristics. So my second point was that because the politics of university professors were freakishly liberal, if diversity of ideas was the goal, then colleges should be aggressively recruiting conservative professors through affirmative action and hiring goals and so on. My college mentor read my essay, threw it over his shoulder, and said, "Fine. Take the flamboyant approach."

Did you get rejected at any law schools?
Yes.

Did you ever hit the wall in law school?
I'm not familiar with the expression, but it doesn't sound good. So no, I don't think so. I was happiest working on *Law Review*: both researching and writing my own notes and reviewing articles submitted to the review.

What was the best advice you ever got?

The best advice about practicing law I ever got was not a single adage, but compact, consistently brilliant editing from Adam Walinsky, the former Bobby Kennedy speech writer who was a partner at one of my law firms. Adam taught me more about writing than anyone I have ever encountered—and cocky associate that I was, I thought I was already a pretty good writer. It was a great working relationship: He mostly left me alone to research, write briefs, and argue cases. But before a brief went out, with just a few minor sweeps of the pen, he could make it sparkle. I learned a lot from him. (In fact, I wish I could find him again so I could start sending him drafts of my books.)

The second-best piece of advice I ever got was from another law-firm partner who explained to me that, in representing a third-party witness in a major case, my objective should be to put off my client's deposition for as long as possible. (The case could settle, they might decide my client's deposition was unnecessary, the plaintiff could die, etc. etc.) He told me I should treat plaintiff's counsel like an unwanted suitor who was the boss's son: return his calls, pretend to be eager and interested, but never actually allow him to set a date.

—ANN COULTER
Columnist and Bestselling Author of
Treason *and other books*

> "It has to ring true."
> —BILL HOYE
> *USC Law School*

that the environment is your passion and expect anyone to take you seriously, not if you've never been involved before. If you say you're committed to public-interest law, show me a record of commitment to the public interest. Everyone I talked to agreed that the worst thing is a phony, and you're dealing with people who are in the business of spotting them a mile away.

Don't try to snow them. Make it real. It doesn't have to be big. One of my most successful students wrote about being a middle child, and connected it with his desire for justice. Pretty good, wouldn't you say? Another wrote about coming from an immigrant family that never trusted lawyers.

Lots of people write about summer jobs. But what about *the* summer job? I need the moment that will convince Joyce Curll that someday you're going to end up on the Supreme Court, or in the Senate, or running for president, or at least running a business or a law firm. The story can take place at a

> Don't waste words or paper repeating what's already there. Respect your reader. He or she has already read the application. They know what's in it. Tell them something new. There's someone just like you who wants the very same slot. Why you?

hamburger stand; she doesn't care if it takes place at the White House—that it's about somebody's father—she cares about the potential of the person. She picked Miguel Estrada. She has to be persuaded that you'll take advantage of Harvard, not be intimidated by it, that you're a leader, not a follower. Right or left doesn't matter. Bill Hoye couldn't care less if you're a right-wing conservative; he's looking for passion.

WRITE WELL. WRITE AS IF YOUR FUTURE DEPENDED ON IT.

We have zero tolerance for grammar and spelling errors. I don't publish my first drafts and I write for a living. Write, then rewrite, then rewrite again. Make it a jewel. Don't make it an encyclopedia. It is much harder to write short than write long. The person who's reading doesn't have time for the phone book. Cut every single extraneous word. Don't spend three paragraphs clearing your throat. Cut to the chase. If the first paragraph doesn't work, it doesn't matter what comes next.

Get someone with good judgment to read and critique it before you send it in. Show them the final draft. Make sure it is neat and clean.

Every single admissions director and admissions committee member whom I talked to gave me chapter and verse about spelling errors, spilled coffee, missing pages, ink stains on applications . . . Rare? Not at all. Common. Spelling errors, especially. Messy applications. "Thats" that should be "which" or "who."

If your application gets read by a faculty member, I promise you that spelling errors and bad grammar are just the sort of thing that could kill you. I know many faculty members who consider such things a personal insult, as in how dare you waste my time, if it wasn't worth your time to get it right.

But don't do some "essay-by-numbers" number either, as in "what I did on my junior year abroad" or, even worse, get someone else to write it for you; I've known faculty members to pull the writing-sample section of the LSAT to see if it reads like the same person. It better . . .

TAILOR IT TO THE SCHOOL.

If the school asks a specific question, ANSWER IT.

Do Research

Find out what the school's strengths are, what, if anything, makes it unique, what they think makes them special.

Show—in a subtle way—that you have done your homework, that your interests match the school's strengths (if they do, remember, it has to be real or close anyway).

Flattery Will Get You Everywhere

Schools are like dates. We all want to feel like we're special to you, and worthy of your attention. We want to be wanted. Don't send everyone the same essay. Don't make the same mistake twice. Sound like a lot of work? So what? Prove to me that you want to get into my school so badly you can taste it . . .

Work me. If it's not personal, not full of passion, if it doesn't make me feel bad about saying no to you, like I'm losing something if I do, it's not working. Start again. Ask your parents' friends what they think makes you special. Think about the class where you've contributed the most. What made your contribution special?

IMPORTANT:
From Bill Hoye,
Dean of Admissions at USC law
PERSONAL STATEMENTS

What doesn't work:

• Skip the travelogue about your summer in Europe. We're all awed when we visit interesting places for the first time. But describing your sense of wonderment is rarely compelling.

• Single space, eight-point font, with no margins. Why make me work hard to get through your statement? Make the formatting easy to read.

• Don't make your personal statement a place for catharsis or therapy. It's absolutely okay (to the extent that you are comfortable) to talk about personal and sensitive issues that have occurred in your life. But the point of doing so will be to show the adversity that you have encountered and, as a result, the perspective that you have gained, and the ability to persevere that you have developed. If this is missing, the reader may have just a very sad story. And that might not work.

• Be careful about making pop-culture references that I likely won't get. I won't understand how song lyrics from the "Mighty Mighty Bosstones" are relevant to your specific life issues. After all, I'm still listening to Fleetwood Mac.

• Creative approaches to your personal statement and application are often fun diversions for the staff, but may not help much. My favorite was the candidate who submitted a take-out box, full of fortune cookies. My job was to break open each fortune cookie, and piece together the various fortunes to form a complete personal statement. It was kind of fun. But, no, the applicant wasn't admitted.

What does work:

• **Excellent writing.** I read thousands of personal statements each year. About every twentieth file, I'll come across a statement that is just a pure pleasure to read. It's just good writing. And that is very important.

• **You get things done.** You're a mover. And you care deeply about what you do. We're a small law school, and I want students who will DO something while they are here and after they leave. But, this is hard to fake because I'll be looking not only at your statement, but also your résumé and at what your recommenders say about you.

• **A personal statement that rings absolutely true.** I believe what I read. Really, I can easily spot an applicant who is trying to portray himself as what he thinks we want him to be rather than who he really is. The personal statement is NOT a place to reinvent yourself. That sort of approach will fail.

• **The statement makes clear that you are sensible, self-possessed, and sophisticated.** Not just starry-eyed.

• **The specific subject in your personal statement doesn't really matter much.** I know that doesn't help an applicant much. But it is true. Whatever you write about, I'll just be looking to see that you are thoughtful and reflective, and that you have learned and grown from your experiences. That you will be intellectually active and engaged in the classroom. And you will be a good classmate to others. You will be fun to teach. You will be stimulating to have around. You'll pursue your interests (as you develop them in law school) passionately and forcefully. *You will enhance the overall intellectual environment of the school.*

HOW TO GET GREAT RECOMMENDATIONS

Great recommendations help a lot. Bad recommendations hurt a lot, and are to be absolutely avoided. Vanilla recommendations (this student got an A in my class, came to class, and did reading) neither help nor hurt and therefore constitute a wasted opportunity.

HOW DO YOU GET A GREAT RECOMMENDATION?

You work at it. Choose wisely.

Consider the wise advice of Bill Hoye on the subject of recommendations:

*"If you attend a large research university, it can be hard to get to know professors. So, a letter from a graduate-student instructor is okay. **But the very best students have really figured out ways to connect with**

faculty during their time in college. Try to be one of those students. Not only will you get a letter of recommendation, but you'll get a better education and will be better prepared for law school.

If you have interned in government, don't spend a lot of time trying to get a letter from the legislator or executive unless she or he is really in a position to evaluate your work in the office. In most cases, it's much better to have the assistant chief of staff or whomever you reported to write the letter. A U.S. senator recently called me on behalf of an applicant. His primary message: "I just wanted you to know that I REALLY meant what I said in my letter of recommendation for this applicant—not like all those other letters that I am pressured into writing." That pretty much sums up the value of most letters from VIPs who may not have worked with you directly.

Avoid a Bad Recommendation at All Costs.

You never want to get a bad recommendation. Ask straight out: Do you feel you could comfortably write me a positive recommendation, which would strengthen my application? If the person can't (or won't) say yes, find someone else. Period.

Think of the package as a whole. The best people to recommend you aren't the most famous people you know, but the ones who know you the best and/or will write the best recommendations. (Okay, some people are jerks about this.)

WHAT DO YOU DO TO GET A GOOD
FACULTY RECOMMENDATION?

• Work hard and suck up during the semester. (Sorry, sad, but true.) Talk in class, do good work, get good grades. Work for a professor. Do research. You don't have to hang around after class or walk the dog.

• Take more than one class from the same professor.

• Choose your adviser wisely. Avoid people who are best avoided. There is a reason that they are avoided. Bad reputations are mostly earned, in my experience.

• Come back and renew (or make) acquaintance with whoever gave you the best grade, or whomever you liked best. Make an appointment, spend time with him/her, impress him/ her, and then give them something to say. Leave them with something in writing.

GIVE YOUR RECOMMENDER
SOMETHING TO SAY.

Don't assume that just because someone knows you and likes you that they have any idea what to say about you. They don't. You need to tell them.

This is especially true, of course, of employers, who don't write these letters for a living.

Do not be insulted when the person says, nicely, "Why don't you write it for me?" View this as an incredible opportunity. Use it wisely and well. For goodness' sake, say yes.

PROVIDE THE RECOMMENDER WITH ALL THE INFORMATION.

I don't care how well he/she knows you, you know yourself better. Think of the key questions that need to be answered and the problems with your package.

What function should this recommendation serve? Be very frank. You need to tell the recommender what you want them to say. They will thank you for it. Never assume they know. You can do it respectfully: "One thing you might like to highlight . . ."; that sort of thing.

At a minimum, a professor's recommendation should serve to answer the question of whether you can do the work. But no one is in a better position than a professor to explain why you bring something extra to class that other students don't— if you can identify what that is, and why they should be buying it.

I spend time with every student for whom I write a recommendation. But many of them can't think of what to tell me. Not good. If they can't impress me, how can I write a letter that will impress someone else?

A recommender can sing your praises in ways that might sound arrogant coming from you: *Were you the one in class who was always willing to stand up for unpopular positions? Who always brought your own experiences into the class?* What family problems have you been forced to deal with that expanded your perspective? Remember, determination matters: How have you demonstrated that you have it? Humor. Courage. Commitment. Sportsmanship. Klutziness, endured with good humor. Impossible parents.

GIVE YOUR RECOMMENDERS PLENTY OF TIME.

Writing recommendations is part of our job as faculty members. Don't apologize. But leave enough time. Do you think that you will get as good a recommendation if you come in to drop off the form one or two days before it's due? No, you'll get vanilla, or maybe worse. ("I'm sorry this recommendation is brief, but the applicant didn't leave me adequate time . . ." I have never done that in my life, but I know people who might, and I know exactly what I would think if I read that.)

> **Don't forget the address and a stamp.** I can't tell you how long my assistant has spent tracking down students who forgot to give us the list of their schools.

If a recommender says to you, "Is there anything else I can do for you?" the answer should always be yes.

- Do they know anyone on the faculty of the law school that is your first choice?
- Can they get you in the door?
- Will they make a call?

I always offer to let students sit in on my classes; most don't take me up on the offer. "Why not?" I think to myself. Aren't they interested? The ones who say yes are more likely to get my attention, get their applications flagged, get me to make calls on their behalf. Why *wouldn't* you ask me for that? Most don't.

{ 8 }

HOW TO GET PERSONAL INTERVIEWS AT SCHOOLS THAT DON'T INTERVIEW

I know. Most law schools say that they don't interview. Except when they do. Which is all the time. Guess what . . .

USC Law School doesn't interview. Except when we do. Bill Hoye explains:

No, formal interviews are not a requirement for our admissions process—except for our Rothman Scholars and candidates for our guaranteed summer jobs. Yet I'll speak to anyone who is interested. I'm surprised how few take me up on the offer—I give out literally thousands of business cards each recruitment season, and hear back from only a handful.

Here is what happens to most candidates. They call our office and ask to speak with me—or maybe they don't know my name but ask for the "dean of admissions." The staff will gently inquire about the nature of the call. Most often, the candidate will say something like "I just have some general questions." Most often, the staff member will say, "Well, maybe I can help." And the hapless candidate will mumble, "Okay . . ."

Other candidates are a bit more savvy. Instead of explaining that she has "general" questions, she will pose a fairly complex and well-thought-out question. What happens then? The staff member transfers the call to me instantly.

Even better, some candidates are even more sophisticated and will have done some homework to discover the name of my assistant. (How hard can that be? It's right on the Web site.) Instead of speaking with the receptionist, the candidate asks to speak directly with my assistant. The call is transferred immediately. Mr. Sophisticated asks my assistant to schedule an interview. My assistant puts the call on hold and tells me that a very professional-sounding and pleasant candidate would like to meet with me. I say, "Sure, find him fifteen minutes."

What happens during a phone or office interview? Well, your file comes to me before our scheduled time. (If it has already been reviewed, it will now get a fresh look. If it has not yet been reviewed, it's now getting some attention.) Remember, this is your time, so I will rarely direct the flow of our conversation. You should consider this meeting as an important test of your advocacy skills. Come very prepared to highlight what you need me to know about your candidacy. Ask smart questions—not questions that can easily be answered by reading the admissions guide. Expect that I will throw one or two questions at you. (You won't be able to guess what they will be, so don't try. They will be designed to get you to think about something from a different perspective, or to consider some countervailing ideas. Just be sure to listen carefully so you can be thoughtful in your response.)

Here is the important thing. After we hang up or you leave my office, I will jot down some notes about our interaction. I might write down some of the questions you asked as an example of your smarts and sophistication. Or, I'll mention the genuine passion you displayed about your interests. Maybe I'll say that you clearly are "better than her numbers." Or, sadly, I might write that there was "nothing special" in the interview.

These notes go directly in your file. And, yes, they can be influential.

HOW DO YOU GET AN INTERVIEW?

If a school offers interviews and you want to go to that school: sign up for an interview. Always make the effort if you possibly can. It will be taken as a sign of your interest. Schools use interviews both as a marketing device and as a measure of interest. If offered an interview, you decline at your peril.

If it's not worth making the effort to interview, you're not going to convince anyone that it's a top choice. If you need money to do it, beg, work, or borrow.

The interview is a critical opportunity.

Some schools actually offer admission during interviews— so if you don't go . . .

Even at those that don't, think about it this way: here's what would happen if you had a very, very rich uncle who called up the dean of the law school to say his nephew was applying. The dean would take the call. He would listen politely, hit your uncle up for money, and tell your uncle they'd consider your application very, very seriously.

The big favor that your uncle would get for all that money is a call to the dean of admissions. "Bob," he'd say, "will you see this kid? Just see him. Do what you think is right once you do." You'd get an interview and a flag. The flag means that the dean finds out before you do whether you're in or not, so he can call your uncle (or avoid him). The interview is your chance to shine.

So what does this mean to you? If you have a rich uncle, or an alumni parent, or a friend in the U.S. Senate, don't use it up on a vanilla recommendation. Try to use it to get an interview. Ask them to help you get in the door. *Clout won't get you in, but it may get you in the door.*

So what about everybody else; those of us who don't have rich uncles, alumni parents, U.S. senators at our beck and call? **You can still get in the door if you try hard enough.**

At most schools, a faculty member can get you in the door. Flattery will get you everywhere. You probably think I get inundated with letters from undergraduates who want to go to law school, have seen me on television, read one of my books, and try flattering me as a way to get in the door. You're wrong. I don't. If I get two or three or four such letters a year, it's a lot. And I'm famous, as law professors go. Most professors get none. See what I mean? Make it a smart letter. Put some work into it.

Or write to the dean of admissions. Say you're coming into town. Specify a narrow window of dates. Ask if you can come in. Ask if you can sit in on a class. Ask if you can come into the office. Ask if you can talk to someone in the office . . .

Find an alumnus/alumna in town. Ask if you can meet with them. Ask if they will get in touch with the admissions office. DO SOME WORK. It's your future.

WHAT DO YOU DO IF YOU GET IN THE DOOR?

Be prepared. Hopefully, this is a top-choice school. The best school that you've got a good chance of getting into in your hometown. Impress everyone you can with:

- Your interest in the school.
- Your commitment to enroll if admitted.
- How smart, together, passionate, and prepared you are, as shown by being on time, pleasant, well-informed, etc.

Rehearse. Know what points you want to make.

Think of an interview as a performance. That does not mean that you simply perform. You still have to listen and interact. What it means is that you have an idea in advance of what points you want to get across . . . what your message is . . . what impression(s) you are trying to convey . . . who your audience(s) is/are.

How do your interests connect with the school's strengths? Which of its top programs are you particularly interested in? Which of its professors do you want to study under? Check the latest news from the law school . . . show that you've done your homework. How do you demonstrate your interests, commitment, etc.?

It should go without saying: Be on time, well-dressed, and polite to everyone. Write a follow-up note thanking people who went out of their way to be helpful to you. A little goes a long way since so few people do anything right at all.

Ask to sit in on a class when you're there. Stay as long as you can. Talk to as many people as you can. Remember, you are trying to impress as many people as you can. If you can't talk to the admissions director, talk to whomever you can in the office. Be unbelievably pleasant. So what if it makes you tense. You are working. Campaigning. Representing your first client. You. Offer to come back again if you have further questions. Yes, it is worth it to get to know these people. They only hold the key to your future. That's all.

{ 9 }

THE CRITICAL
IMPORTANCE OF
FOLLOW-THROUGH

Take absolutely nothing for granted. Assume no one does what they say they'll do. Check back. Be nice to assistants. Make sure your package is complete early. It does you no good to do your work early if your recommenders don't.

I know of lots of cases where my office can't get recommendations in because the students leave for Christmas break without giving us the right forms and we can't find them. Or the list of schools. Or I've asked for a résumé and writing sample and they simply never provided one. And I'm supposed to be recommending them. What can I say? Doesn't follow directions. Doesn't follow through. I know how to write a vanilla recommendation, and sometimes I do it on purpose. I think to myself, "Why would you do this if you want me to think well of you?"

The way that you handle the application process is part of your application. If you have your parents do any part of it, you lose points.

You should be doing this yourself, start to finish. Not having Mom or Dad call the office, schedule an interview, etc. Believe me, not doing it yourself will actually hurt you.

There is no such thing as a nonevaluative interaction with the admissions office. We evaluate everything, even the way that the applicant treats the receptionist. I have denied admission, or placed on a waiting list, many a wonderful intellect who did not treat the admissions-office staff with respect and decorum. Please note: most admissions offices are very small, and we get to know our applicant pool very well, as well as each other. If someone stands outside the standard deviation in terms of behavior or language, that person will stand out. You just better be very sure on which end (the good end or the bad end) of the standard-deviation graph your behavior or language puts you.

You can't use parents or spouses as your spokespeople. The average age of our entering class is twenty-five years. This means that most of our applicants have been out of school for approximately two to four years. Applicants who are applying to law school should be able to manage this process, both its frustrations and victories, by themselves. Besides, state and federal privacy laws prevent us from sharing a lot of information with anyone (including parents, relatives, and friends), other than the applicant. Having parents assist students with the search for the undergraduate institution is understandable. When an applicant begins the application process for graduate school, it is time for the parents to step aside.

—COLLINS BYRD, University of Minnesota

Never, ever, ever be rude to anyone in the admissions office. Not a secretary, not a receptionist, not a student guide, not the security guard.

You Will Not Get In.

I Don't Care What Your Numbers Are. Period. Promise.

RUN YOUR OWN CAMPAIGN.

Maybe law school will come to you. Maybe life has. Maybe the LSAT did. But somewhere along the way, maybe sooner or maybe later, you will discover that the most successful people aren't the ones with the best grades or the best numbers or the best scores: they end up being the ones who go for it in the very biggest way and keep going for it and, of course, are shrewd and lucky. But it's going for it that counts as much as the numbers. Numbers are for lazy people who don't put themselves on the line, and they only take you so far. Rely on them too long and they'll spoil you. Maybe now, maybe for your first job, maybe for your fifth. But sooner or later, you have to rely on you. Decide what you want most. Be willing to go for it.

Run a campaign to get it.

I have never heard anyone else describe it this way, but believe me, I have seen it done, I have helped students do it, and I've done it myself more than a few times. Twenty years ago, I went door-to-door to get my friend Jack Corrigan into Harvard Law School; at that time, I worked each member of the admissions committee personally to explain his somewhat interrupted undergraduate record (that's putting it nicely) as well as his political genius. In the years since, I have managed a few successful efforts that I can't describe, for obvious reasons, except in the most generic terms.

Let's say that there's one school that you want to attend, above all others. Your numbers are close, bottom side of the median . . . just inside the ballpark, but just. But it's the city where you want to practice, the place where you want to be; it's USC in Los Angeles, or Georgetown in D.C., or Penn in Philadelphia, or NYU in New York . . . You want it so badly you can almost taste it; you've wanted it for years now. And then you take the LSAT and you feel like your dreams have just gone up in smoke.

Do you give up? Did Bill Clinton give up when people said that George Bush couldn't be beat? No. Did Harry Truman give up when they said that Dewey had it won? No. They ran campaigns. You can, too. Subtle campaigns. Determined campaigns. Smart campaigns. What have you got to lose?

Focus on the school. How are you going to show that you have something extra, supersparkle, just what they need? Who are you working for? Who is your favorite professor? Look at your assets. Who in your office, school, community, went there? Get the interview. Write the letter. Do the reading. Let them know, in no uncertain terms, not only that it's your first-choice school, but why. Make it convincing. Come to sit in on a class. Go see the admissions director. Plead your case in person. Find a member of the faculty who went to your undergraduate college, played the sport you do, shares your interest in wild bees, trumpet playing, politics, whatever it is that you do. Ask for your mother's help.

Politely, pleasantly, keep following up. Don't expect it to work right away. Step one is to at least get yourself wait-listed instead of rejected. This is what "Joel" (not his real name) did. His mother asked me for help. Don't even ask how she knew me. Nothing fancy. Believe me, I'm certain he didn't want to ask his mother, and she didn't want to ask me, but this is no time for pride. I gave his mother my e-mail address and he wrote me a smart, funny, self-deprecating letter. I invited him to come see me during office hours on his next trip home. He did. He shared my interest in politics. Step one.

He was working. Someone in his office had gone to USC. It hadn't occurred to him that this fellow could really help. After all, he was only a young alum, not a big giver, not a famous person. Doesn't matter. I urged him to urge the alum to get in touch with the dean of admissions so there would be two of us on the case, at least one of whom knew him well (the alum). He did. WE did. He stayed on top of things. His boss turned out to be active in alumni activities (and got more active as a result of getting involved in Joel's case).

Joel got on the waiting list. Most people who get on the waiting list promptly give up. Never hear from them again. Decide that means they've been rejected. Not our Joel. He called me. What should he do now? Go back and see the dean of admissions again, I said. Tell him you'll be there even if you hear the hour before. He did.

WAIT-LISTED

You're on the wait list and you really want to come. What do you do? First, if you are applying right from college, be sure that you submit your spring-semester transcripts (and fall semester, if you didn't send those earlier) to LSAC. LSAC will recompute your GPA and your GPA percentile ranking (how you ranked against your peers who are also applying from your college). I will rarely admit someone off the wait list who has not submitted ALL of his or her college grades. (What is he hiding?)

Use this opportunity to submit a couple additional letters of recommendation, if there are others who can write very positive things about you.

Most important, keep in touch with us. Send a well-written e-mail or a fax every few weeks throughout the summer. If it is true, tell us that we're your number one choice. That you'll be here in an instant, even if the offer comes right before school starts. If space opens up in August, we may not have the time to try to figure out who is still in- terested in enrolling. It's vital to have some recent communication in your file.

—BILL HOYE, *Dean of Admissions, USC Law*

Let the admissions office know what you've been doing in the months since your original application. Give them an update. No one else does. Make sure you keep in touch with your "rabbis," letting everyone involved know that you haven't lost interest. Do you need to know what happened next to our Joel? He got accepted in August. The moral of this story: Determination is one of the things that make a lawyer. It's as important, in many respects, as the gray matter. It's how we justify the LSAT business, and it's also rewarded in the ad- missions process. So is hard work. Not only did Joel get in, but he turned out to be a great student. Graduates this year.

I was stunned, when my students and I did the surveys for this book, at the variations in how much time students put into their law school applications. Most students put in very little time. "Easy," more than one said. Just think what an advantage it can be for you to put in more time than most.

Should you tell a school if it's your first choice? Yes. Remember: Flattery will get you everywhere in life. Also, some ratings systems used to count in yield (what percent of the students who accepted have enrolled), and while the big- gies have abandoned it, others still count it. Ego is big in this business.

So why not tell everyone that they're your first choice? Because these people are pros. They spot phonies. *"It has to ring true."* Bill Hoye's words. Any campaign should be focused, selective, and sincere. Otherwise it will backfire. Bad to get a bad reputation before you've even begun. You're dealing with very, very smart people.

{ 10 }

HOW TO TARGET YOUR APPLICATIONS TO THE RIGHT SCHOOLS FOR YOU

"What law school do you want to go to?"

"The best one I get into."

WRONG ANSWER.

At least if you define "best" the way that everyone else does.

This is the other half of the numbers game, and students are also its victims. They are desperate to get into a "national" law school, a T14 law school, a school that is up two points from last year. It's bad enough that the schools fall for this stuff. You don't have to.

WHY YOU SHOULDN'T GO TO THE "BEST" LAW SCHOOL THAT YOU GET INTO

HOW EVERYONE ELSE DEFINES "BEST"

In 1987, *U.S. News & World Report* started ranking law schools. In the first year, they ranked only twenty. Harvard and Yale tied for first. Big surprise. In the first survey, ninety-six law school deans were asked to list what they considered the country's top ten schools. Six years later, *U.S. News* expanded its rankings to include all the accredited law schools in the country; it ranked the top twenty-five schools and assigned the rest to quartiles. The current system ranks the "top" one hundred schools, and divides the remaining seventy-seven schools into the third and fourth tiers, which aren't ranked; nine more schools aren't on the list because their accreditation is pending.

The law schools are united in condemning the ratings. If you apply to law school, you'll get a letter signed by ninety deans in April, including most of the top law schools in the country, the same month the *U.S. News* ratings come out, stating that the rating system "ignores the qualities that make you and law schools unique."

There are plenty of things wrong with the *U.S. News* rankings, as Professor Brian Leiter explains on his Web site. Asking about reputation helps old schools in the Northeast, where lawyers are concentrated, and per-student expenditures help small schools. Some factors, like diversity and student satisfaction, aren't considered at all. Others depend entirely on what the schools themselves report. Some numbers are fishy: accord-

RANK	CATEGORY	WEIGHT
\multicolumn{3}{c}{**AMERICA'S BEST LAW SCHOOLS RANKINGS ARE BASED ON TWELVE CRITERIA**}		
1	Median LSAT scores	12.50%
2	Median undergrad GPA	10%
3	Fall acceptance rate	2.50%
4	Law school faculty surveys	25%
5	Lawyer/judge surveys	15%
6	Employment at graduation	6%
7	Employment after nine months	12%
8	Bar passage rate	2%
9	Average per-student instructional expenditures	9.75%
10	Student/faculty ratio	3%
11	Average per-student expenditures on noninstructional items (like financial aid)	1.50%
12	Volumes in the library	0.75%

ing to the self-reports, Harvard actually has more students unemployed nine months after graduation than Duke, which, if true, may be a reflection of the number of screenwriters in the class, not the quality of the education.

Then there's the matter of manipulation. While the schools outdo one another in condemning the ratings, the fact is that, internally, they take them incredibly seriously. If you're trying to impress alums, raise money for your school, get money from the provost or the university president, further your career as a dean, and prove that you deserve to go on to be a university president, it helps (a lot) to show that your ratings are going up. By contrast, it is very bad, in terms of internal politics and external recruitment, to have your ratings going down. It's a self-fulfilling prophecy; even if the rankings mean nothing, the fact that students rely on them, alumni read about them, administrators respond to them, and would-be faculty hear about them makes them real.

So you can hate them or view them as meaningless, but you ignore them at your peril. Most schools don't ignore them. Quite the contrary. There is endless gossip about what schools do to manipulate their ratings. I don't believe all of it. Just most of it.

Examples: Some schools would rather have students who have either very high LSATs or very high grades rather than a balance because they're looking to up their medians. So they'll reject "better" students in favor of those with more skewed numbers to improve their own. One school supposedly created a part-time night program for students with lower numbers to improve its medians, since only full-time students are considered in formulating medians. Some schools reportedly waive fees for students with no chance of getting in to make themselves look more selective.

Some schools go to great lengths to publicize themselves, knowing that some of the people getting the "ads" are the raters for the rankings.

Schools put unemployed graduates on their own payrolls so that they are "employed," even if it is only as research assistants and such, so as to boost their numbers.

Deans from some top schools don't vote for one another to gain competitive advantage. Horrors—law school leaders doing such things, but, of course, they do not care a bit . . . Right.

U.S. News isn't the only one doing ratings these days. Other sources include Professor Leiter, whose results I'll give you below; *American Lawyer*, which only surveys major law firms for their ratings; and a number of authors selling books, who attack *U.S. News* and then do their own rankings, which tend to be worse, or at least more idiosyncratic, and in many cases very questionable. I told you about the one that didn't put UCLA in the top forty (inexplicable); I was told of another that ranked Georgetown ahead of Chicago, which I don't buy at all, even though Georgetown is a very good school.

But lots of people do. This is what is striking. In researching this book, I have come to understand that ratings play a bigger role in the lives of students, mostly for the worse, than I thought. Students not only give the ratings more significance than they deserve, they incorporate them into their self-esteem.

The fundamental premise of the ratings is that you have to decide between 186 (or so) law schools, and you should go to the "best" of those (measured by somebody's ratings system) that you get into.

That is simply untrue for most people. First of all, most people simply aren't free to go live anywhere in the entire fifty states, nor do they want to, if they could. Second, if you could, you shouldn't, unless you really have no idea either where you want to live, or where you want to work, or even what you want to do afterward.

In other words, the hypothetical matchups between a school where you might go and the one where you have no interest don't matter. Whether your first-choice school is number twelve in one survey and number eighteen in another is the sort of bragging that I warn my ten-year-old against. It's still your first choice. And rightly so, if you plan to settle in that city, and it's the best law school there, and you're not getting into Harvard, Yale, Stanford.

Where do you want to live? To practice?

15 LARGEST METROPOLITAN AREAS

	METRO. AREA POPULATION (2000 CENSUS)[1]	CITY POPULATION (2000 CENSUS)[2]	NUMBER OF LAWYERS/LAW OFFICES IN METRO AREA (2001)[3]	MEDIAN ANNUAL SALARY FOR LAWYERS (2002)[4]	OVERALL COST OF LIVING (COMPARED TO THE NATIONAL AVERAGE)[5]
New York	21,199,865 (#1)	8,008,278 (#1)	83,146/6,403	$126,300	193.4%
Los Angeles	16,373,645 (#2)	3,694,820 (#2)	45,230/6,927	$107,100	140.0%
Chicago	9,157,540 (#3)	2,896,016 (#3)	25,000–49,999/ 5,554	$98,400	112.0%
Washington DC	7,608,070 (#4)	572,059 (#21)	49,093/4,000	$107,000	127.7%
San Francisco	7,039,362 (#5)	776,733 (#13)	22,126/2,019	$135,000	217.0%
Philadelphia	6,188,463 (#6)	1,517,550 (#5)	25,000–49,999/ 3,537	$90,600	97.1%
Boston	5,819,100 (#7)	589,141 (#20)	30,987/4,666	$76,700	132.0%
Detroit	5,456,428 (#8)	951,270 (#10)	16,715/2,625	$65,700	88.5%
Dallas	5,221,801 (#9)	1,188,580 (#8)	18,426/2,378	$107,300	104.2%
Houston	4,669,571 (#10)	1,953,631 (#4)	10,000–24,999/ 2,975	$131,100	95.4%
Atlanta	4,112,198 (#11)	416,474 (#40)	10,000–24,999/ 2,742	$80,300	109.4%

[1] Mack J. Perry & Paul J. Mackun, *Population Change and Distribution: 1990–2000,* U.S. Census 2000, p. 2 (April 2001), available at http://www.census.gov/prod/2001pubs/c2kbr01-2.pdf.

[2] *Id.*

[3] 2001 MSA Business Patterns (NAICS), U.S. Census Bureau, available at http://censtats.census.gov/cbpnaic/cbpnaic.shtml.

[4] America's Career InfoNet: Metro Wages, available at http://www.acinet.org/acinet.

[5] Sperling's Best Places, available at http://www.bestplaces.net.

15 LARGEST METROPOLITAN AREAS (cont.)				
	METRO. AREA POPULATION (2000 CENSUS)[1]	CITY POPULATION (2000 CENSUS)[2]	NUMBER OF LAWYERS/LAW OFFICES IN METRO AREA (2001)[3]	MEDIAN ANNUAL SALARY FOR LAWYERS (2002)[4]	OVERALL COST OF LIVING (COMPARED TO THE NATIONAL AVERAGE)[5]
Miami	3,876,380 (#12)	362,470 (#48)	16,437/2,995	$96,500	112.3%
Seattle	3,554,760 (#13)	563,374 (#24)	13,585/1,852	$82,300	136.3%
Phoenix	3,251,876 (#14)	1,321,045 (#6)	10,000–24,999/ 1,706	$70,900	101.8%
Minneapolis	2,968,806 (#15)	382,618 (#46)	10,000–24,999/ 1,675	$88,400	104.7%

As for your second choice, it may as well be the second-best law school in that very same city. Viewing it as second tier will only make you feel bad about yourself and risk insulting faculty and alumni when you meet them.

Your third choice might be the third best: if you want to practice in Los Angeles, you might be applying to USC, UCLA, Loyola, and Pepperdine; you might go a little bit out of town and start looking at Davis and Hastings, but does it matter how Northwestern is doing this year or if Wisconsin is up or down, if you're planning to practice in L.A. and stay in L.A.? And just to keep you studying, every one of these schools has a median LSAT within about eight or nine points.

With only 185 law schools, there are more talented would-be professors than schools for them to teach at. If you think that the competition to attend is tough, imagine the competition to teach. As with so many other things in life, what you get out of law school has a lot to do with what you put in.

LAW SCHOOLS NEAR THE 15 LARGEST METROPOLITAN AREAS

METROPOLITAN AREA	NEARBY ABA ACCREDITED LAW SCHOOLS	U.S. NEWS RANKING: 2004[6]/ 2003[7]/ 2002[8]	SCHOOL'S BAR PASSAGE RATE/ STATEWIDE BAR PASSAGE RATE[9]	STUDENTS EMPLOYED 9 MONTHS AFTER GRADUATION[10]
NEW YORK	Columbia University	4/4/4	93.2% / 76% (NY)	100.0%
	New York University	5/5/5	95.5% / 76% (NY)	100.0%
	Fordham University	31/32/32	91.5% / 76% (NY)	94.9%
	Benjamin N. Cardozo	57/ Second Tier/ Second Tier	81.9% / 76% (NY)	97.9%
	Brooklyn Law School	59/ Second Tier/ Second Tier	81.1% / 76% (NY)	97.9%
	St. John's University	69/ Second Tier/ Second Tier	79.7% / 76% (NY)	99.3%
	Pace University (White Plains, NY)	Third Tier/ Third Tier/ Third Tier	64.8% / 76% (NY)	91.5%
	New York Law School	Third Tier/ Third Tier/ Fourth Tier	69.5% / 76% (NY)	91.3%
	Hofstra University (Hempstead, NY)	Third Tier/ Third Tier/ Third Tier	76.4% / 76% (NY)	94.2%

(continued)

[6] Best Graduate Schools 2004, Schools of Law, *U.S. News & World Report,* Vol. 134, No. 12, p. 70 (April 14, 2003).

[7] Best Graduate Schools 2003, Schools of Law, *U.S. News & World Report,* Vol. 132, No. 12, p. 64 (April 15, 2002).

[8] Best Graduate Schools 2002, Schools of Law, *U.S. News & World Report,* Vol. 130, No. 14, p. 78 (April 9, 2001).

[9] Best Graduate Schools 2004.

[10] Id.

LAW SCHOOLS NEAR THE 15 LARGEST METROPOLITAN AREAS

METROPOLITAN AREA	NEARBY ABA ACCREDITED LAW SCHOOLS	*U.S. NEWS* RANKING: 2004[6]/ 2003[7]/ 2002[8]	SCHOOL'S BAR PASSAGE RATE/ STATEWIDE BAR PASSAGE RATE[9]	STUDENTS EMPLOYED 9 MONTHS AFTER GRADUATION[10]
	City University of New York at Queens College	Fourth Tier/ Fourth Tier/ Fourth Tier	65.8% / 76% (NY)	74.5%
	Touro College (Huntington, NY)	Fourth Tier/ Fourth Tier/ Fourth Tier	58.2% / 76% (NY)	84.1%
LOS ANGELES	University of California Los Angeles	16/16/16	90.8% / 66% (CA)	96.9%
	University of Southern California	18/18/18	81.7% / 66% (CA)	100.0%
	Loyola Law School	69/ Second Tier/ Third Tier	79% / 66% (CA)	97.1%
	Pepperdine University (Malibu, CA)	Third Tier/ Third Tier/ Third Tier	71.4% / 66% (CA)	85.8%
	Southwestern University	Third Tier/ Third Tier/ Third Tier	68% / 66% (CA)	95.6%
	Chapman University (Orange, CA)	Third Tier/ Not ranked/ Not ranked	63.6% / 66% (CA)	93.8%
	Whittier Law School (Costa Mesa, CA)	Fourth Tier/ Fourth Tier/ Fourth Tier	46.8% / 66% (CA)	92.5%
	Western State University College of Law (Fullerton, CA)	Not ranked/ Not ranked/ Not ranked	N/A	N/A
CHICAGO	University of Chicago	6/6/6	98.4% / 83% (IL)	99.5%
	Northwestern University	12/11/13	95.3% / 83% (IL)	98.6%

METROPOLITAN AREA	NEARBY ABA ACCREDITED LAW SCHOOLS	U.S. NEWS RANKING: 2004[6]/ 2003[7]/ 2002[8]	SCHOOL'S BAR PASSAGE RATE/ STATEWIDE BAR PASSAGE RATE[9]	STUDENTS EMPLOYED 9 MONTHS AFTER GRADUATION[10]
	Loyola University Chicago	69/ Second Tier/ Second Tier	90.8% / 83% (IL)	97.9%
	Illinois Institute of Technology (Chicago–Kent)	69/ Second Tier/ Second Tier	78.1% / 83% (IL)	94.9%
	DePaul University College of Law	Third Tier/ Third Tier/ Third Tier	73.6% / 83% (IL)	83.2%
	Valparaiso University (Valparaiso, IN)	Third Tier/ Fourth Tier/ Third Tier	72.9% / 79% (IN)	95.4%
	Northern Illinois University College of Law (De Kalb, IL)	Fourth Tier/ Third Tier/ Third Tier	74.7% / 83% (IL)	91.7%
	The John Marshall Law School	Fourth Tier/ Fourth Tier/ Fourth Tier	69.1% / 83% (IL)	85.7%
WASHINGTON, D.C.	Georgetown University Law Center	14/14/14	95.3% / 76% (NY)	98.6%
	George Washington University Law School	22/25/23	89.9% / 76% (NY)	98.6%
	George Mason University (Arlington, VA)	40/47/47	69% / 73% (VA)	98.5%
	American University	55/49/ Second Tier	69.6% / 72% (MD)	94.6%
	The Catholic University of America	84/Third Tier/ Second Tier	65.3% / 72% (MD)	93.9%
	Howard University	Third Tier/ Third Tier/ Fourth Tier	68.8% / 76% (NY)	88.3%

(continued)

LAW SCHOOLS NEAR THE 15 LARGEST METROPOLITAN AREAS

METROPOLITAN AREA	NEARBY ABA ACCREDITED LAW SCHOOLS	U.S. NEWS RANKING: 2004[6]/ 2003[7]/ 2002[8]	SCHOOL'S BAR PASSAGE RATE/ STATEWIDE BAR PASSAGE RATE[9]	STUDENTS EMPLOYED 9 MONTHS AFTER GRADUATION[10]
	University of the District of Columbia	Not ranked/ Not ranked/ Not ranked	N/A	N/A
SAN FRANCISCO	Stanford University	2/2/2	92.4% / 66% (CA)	98.9%
	University of California Berkeley	10/7/9	89.7% / 66% (CA)	98.3%
	University of California Hastings	37/40/36	82.2% / 66% (CA)	94.4%
	Santa Clara University	91/ Second Tier/ Third Tier	82% / 66% (CA)	90.0%
	University of San Francisco	97/ Third Tier/ Third Tier	72% / 66% (CA)	91.8%
	Golden Gate University	Fourth Tier/ Fourth Tier/ Fourth Tier	54% / 66% (CA)	78.1%
PHILADELPHIA	University of Pennsylvania	7/7/10	95.5% / 76% (NY)	100.0%
	Temple University	64/ Second Tier/ Second Tier	74.3% / 76% (PA)	91.2%
	Villanova University	69/ Second Tier/ Second Tier	82% / 76% (PA)	94.0%
	Rutgers State University (Camden, NJ)	78/ Second Tier/ Second Tier	69.5% / 73% (NJ)	93.9%
BOSTON	Harvard Law School (Cambridge, MA)	3/3/3	95.5% / 76% (NY)	99.0%
	Boston College	22/22/22	94.1% / 81% (MA)	97.6%

LAW SCHOOLS NEAR THE 15 LARGEST METROPOLITAN AREAS

METROPOLITAN AREA	NEARBY ABA ACCREDITED LAW SCHOOLS	*U.S. NEWS* RANKING: 2004[6]/ 2003[7]/ 2002[8]	SCHOOL'S BAR PASSAGE RATE / STATEWIDE BAR PASSAGE RATE[9]	STUDENTS EMPLOYED 9 MONTHS AFTER GRADUATION[10]
	Boston University	28/25/27	88.4% / 81% (MA)	99.7%
	Northeastern University	89/ Third Tier/ Third Tier	84.8% / 81% (MA)	91.9%
	Suffolk University	Third Tier/ Fourth Tier/ Fourth Tier	77.3% / 81% (MA)	93.9%
	New England School of Law	Fourth Tier/ Fourth Tier/ Fourth Tier	71.5% / 81% (MA)	83.3%
DETROIT	University of Michigan–Ann Arbor	7/7/7	89.7% / 76% (NY)	98.7%
	Wayne State University Law School	97/ Third Tier/ Third Tier	81.6% / 76% (MI)	97.3%
	University of Detroit Mercy	Fourth Tier/ Fourth Tier/ Fourth Tier	81.3% / 76% (MI)	90.9%
DALLAS	Southern Methodist University	50/49/47	87.3% / 81% (TX)	95.1%
	Texas Wesleyan University (Fort Worth, TX)	Fourth Tier/ Fourth Tier/ Fourth Tier	76.7% / 81% (TX)	91.3%
HOUSTON	University of Houston Law Center	69/ Second Tier/ 50	91.5% / 81% (TX)	88.8%
	South Texas College of Law	Fourth Tier/ Fourth Tier/ Fourth Tier	79% / 81% (TX)	80.8%
	Texas Southern University	Fourth Tier/ Fourth Tier/ Fourth Tier	N/A	N/A

(continued)

LAW SCHOOLS NEAR THE 15 LARGEST METROPOLITAN AREAS

METROPOLITAN AREA	NEARBY ABA ACCREDITED LAW SCHOOLS	U.S. NEWS RANKING: 2004[6]/ 2003[7]/ 2002[8]	SCHOOL'S BAR PASSAGE RATE/ STATEWIDE BAR PASSAGE RATE[9]	STUDENTS EMPLOYED 9 MONTHS AFTER GRADUATION[10]
ATLANTA	Emory University	27/22/27	93.8% / 85% (GA)	98.0%
	Georgia State University College of Law	91/ Second Tier/ Second Tier	91.4% / 85% (GA)	92.5%
	University of Georgia (Athens, GA)	31/32/27	92.1% / 85% (GA)	97.0%
MIAMI	University of Miami (Coral Gables, FL)	84/ Second Tier/ Second Tier	83.3% / 79% (FL)	90.5%
	St. Thomas University	Fourth Tier/ Fourth Tier/ Fourth Tier	73.3% / 79% (FL)	90.0%
	Nova Southeastern University (Ft. Lauderdale, FL)	Fourth Tier/ Fourth Tier/ Fourth Tier	N/A	N/A
SEATTLE	University of Washington	45/25/23	82.4% / 76% (WA)	75.0%
	Seattle University	91/ Fourth Tier/ Third Tier	76.9% / 76% (WA)	99.3%
PHOENIX	University of Arizona (Tucson, AZ)	44/40/40	81.4% / 78% (AZ)	93.7%
	Arizona State University (Tempe, AZ)	59/ Second Tier/ Second Tier	91.3% / 78% (AZ)	88.7%
MINNEAPOLIS	University of Minnesota	19/18/19	93.9%	97.5%
	William Mitchell College of Law (St. Paul, MN)	Third Tier/ Third Tier/ Third Tier	86.7% / 90% (MN)	93.3%
	Hamline University (St. Paul, MN)	Fourth Tier/ Fourth Tier/ Fourth Tier	85.8% / 90% (MN)	90.7%

Barry Scheck, the nation's authority on the death penalty and forensic evidence, teaches at Cardozo Law School, not one of the top ten. Nadine Strossen, the president of the ACLU, teaches at New York Law School. Ditto. Great teachers, by the way. Why? Because they want/need to live in New York. Laurie Levenson, who is a great criminal-law professor and CBS talking head, teaches at Loyola in L.A. You can be challenged anywhere you go.

I have found in the application process more snobbery than I ever would have predicted. It is generally not from people who know anything about law. It is often from mothers. I say this with some reluctance for all of the obvious reasons, but there it is. Perhaps it is the aftermath of what has been happening at the nursery school level in large cities. Don't let it destroy your life.

Also, don't let it get in the way of making the connections that you need. I saw all these students dumping on their own law schools online and in my own survey responses. I thought, "I'm glad I didn't go to that law school." Alumni do not like thinking of their alma mater as second rate or third tier. They don't refer to it that way. Neither do the faculty. If you're embarrassed by it, you make everyone uncomfortable. Don't apologize for where you're going. Don't compare yourself to other people. How good a lawyer you are does not correlate with the *U.S. News & World Report* ranking of your law school. Many great lawyers were trained and tried cases before the non-lawyers at *U.S. News* invented their system. Stand tall. Decide you're going to be your best, do your best on your terms, or don't do it. Who would want you for their lawyer if you were anything less?

No reason to be a snob, I said to one snobby mom as she explained to me why her son wasn't interested in Loyola Law

School (157/162; 3.1/3.6). I patiently explained to her that she would be lucky if her son got in. Ultimately, he did, enjoyed Loyola, graduated, and got a very good job. Five years from now, people will ask him where he works, not where he went to law school. By the way, he had a lot of great professors. Some of whom could probably teach at "better" law schools, but for a variety of reasons, they have to live in L.A., so they teach at Loyola. But then you go on a Web site and hear students referring to their schools and themselves as "second tier" and "third rate" because that is how *U.S. News* ranks them.

What I want to tell you, first and foremost, is that the law school that you attend and its rank is far more important in your own little world than in the much larger one in which I live. You're not in the real world right now. Know that. What you think is important isn't. Third tier. T14. Normal lawyers have no idea what you're talking about. I did a survey of a dozen high-powered lawyers I know. All of them had gone to "T14" schools. Not one of them knew what it meant. Know that. It should be a relief. It will be someday.

When you get outside of academics, beyond your first job and the largest law firms, your career is increasingly up to you and increasingly influenced by your work experience. People don't spend their lives at their first jobs anymore. Is there any job where you would want to spend your entire life?

{ 11 }

HOW YOU SHOULD DEFINE "BEST" FOR YOURSELF

At the very top. This is easy. Who's on top? They fight about it. Does anyone care? Does it matter?

Harvard Law School, Yale Law School, and Stanford Law School. Or, Yale, Harvard, Stanford; or, Stanford, Yale, Harvard . . . or whatever . . .

Do them in whatever order you want. Spend all day fighting about it. THESE ARE GREAT, GREAT LAW SCHOOLS. CONGRATULATIONS IF YOU'VE GOT

25%–75% PERCENTILE LSAT & GPA SCORES		
SCHOOL	LSAT	GPA
Stanford University	168–170	3.67–3.93
Yale Law School	168–174	3.75–3.97
Harvard Law School	167–173	3.76–3.94

Information found at www.lsac.org

A CHANCE. WORK LIKE CRAZY TO MAXIMIZE. REALLY WORK ON THAT APPLICATION. SHOW THAT YOU'RE A LEADER. If those are your choices (lucky you) ask yourself:

- East or West?
- Big or Small?
- Campus or City?
- Dorm or Apartment?

You can get exactly the same jobs whichever you choose. Your education depends in large part on you, especially at Harvard. In retrospect, I'm glad that I went to Harvard because of my classmates—the future rulers of the world—as opposed to considerations of location, faculty/student ratio (terrible at the time), facilities (the smallest dorm room in creation), etc.

These schools typically still give money based on need; you can play them off against schools in the next batch and get more money from those schools, but the last time that I checked, they were the last vestiges of need-blind admissions and need-based aid.

NOTE: You will not automatically get into all three because you have high numbers. All of them get more applications from people with top numbers than they can possibly expect. So they expect more. Remember, there are lots of people with numbers just as high; don't take anything for granted.

EXTRA NOTE: If you don't have the numbers or something extraordinary in your favor, don't bother. Knowing someone, yes, even me, won't get you in. I have to explain this to my own friends all the time. I cannot get their children in even if my best friend is the dean. If you don't have the numbers for these schools, you are not going to get in, so why waste your time and morale, and set yourself up for the rapid return of little thin slips of paper, not to mention using up favors from people better saved for better things?

WHERE WOULD I GO AMONG THESE THREE?

A few years ago, I would have said Stanford hands-down, because my friend Kathleen was dean and she was building, not to mention the tech boom. Kathleen is stepping down next year, while Harvard and Yale just named new deans, Elena Kagan and Harold Koh, both young (to me) and smart. Koh's vision of the future, like mine, is that the world is the stage. Then again, there's still the future-leaders-of-the-world argument: Every day I turn around and say, "Oh, I went to law school, in Harvard's favor, with him." Unfortunately, it is mostly still him. Not her. But that was my last book.

The next three are:

The University of Chicago, Columbia University, and New York University.

25%–75% PERCENTILE LSAT & GPA SCORES		
SCHOOL	LSAT	GPA
University of Chicago	167–171	3.54–3.76
Columbia University	166–173	3.51–3.85
New York University	168–172	3.50–3.81

Information found at www.lsac.org

Do these three in any order you want to. If I were going to law school myself today, I'd probably put NYU first—but that is because my friend John Sexton, as dean of NYU, and now president of the university, was and is a superstar. He raised a ton of money, recruited faculty, and moved NYU into the top tier. It has a reputation, well deserved, as more public interest oriented than other schools. Norman Dorsen has been working the international side with his usual brilliance and energy.

Chicago may have, pound for pound, the best faculty anywhere. By that measure, it may be the "best" law school. Politically, it's more conservative. It's colder. More intense. Very academic.

A few years ago, people were scared off from New York by 9/11. Now, as they say, absolutely everybody applies to NYU and Columbia. Some people are scared off by Chicago's reputation as being conservative, and by the cold. I can't speak for the cold, except to say that Chicago is a great city with great food, if that helps, and you're inside for the first year studying anyway, so what difference does it make if it's cold? Rumor has it that Chicago is playing with money for students it wants, even though they deny it, because it has to, because Northwestern is. So if you don't mind the cold, it is one incredible opportunity.

THE T14, AND ALL THAT JAZZ

What's the T14? This is very big among students. It's the list of the fourteen schools that have made the top fourteen in the *U.S. News* list since they started compiling it. Basically, it's the six schools listed above, plus the next eight:

University of Michigan

University of Pennsylvania

University of Virginia

Cornell University

Berkeley (Boalt Hall)

Duke University

Northwestern University

Georgetown University

25%–75% PERCENTILE LSAT & GPA SCORES

SCHOOL	LSAT	GPA
University of Michigan	163–168	3.43–3.77
University of Pennsylvania	165–168	3.37–3.76
University of Virginia	164–168	3.49–3.78
Cornell University	164–166	3.50–3.79
UC Berkeley (Boalt)	161–168	3.68–3.9
Duke University	164–169	3.34–3.76
Northwestern University	165–169	3.3–3.7
Georgetown University	165–169	3.48–3.79

Information found at www.lsac.org

Now, are those fourteen better than Texas? Not if you ask anyone from Texas. If you got into Texas and Northwestern and you were planning to practice in Dallas, where should you go? That's not even a hard question . . . Texas.

Are the T14 schools better than USC or UCLA? Not if you ask anyone from L.A.

Better than the University of Wisconsin? Don't ask folks in Milwaukee.

Virginia over Minnesota? Don't tell people in Minneapolis. See what I mean? It depends.

Duke has a terrific new dean, but Professor Leiter thinks that it is overrated (even if they've succeeded in luring my friend Erwin Chemerinsky, a huge addition to the faculty), and so do a lot of people in academics. Georgetown just went through a crisis with its longtime, fabulous dean, who is now stepping down. My friend Christopher Edley has just been named dean of Berkeley, which I think is a great thing for that school, signaling an exciting period of growth and activity after what has been the painful embarrassment of an alleged sexual-harassment scandal involving the former dean and a student. Deans matter because they have a lot to do with the "success" of the law school, including how much money there will be both from the university and private donors for scholarships (a big deal from a student's point of view), faculty (should be a big deal), expensive programs, etc. Deanships change often since it's a really hard job and being a professor is such a pleasant and easy job; the ones who like it and are good become college presidents very quickly. So most deans do their jobs and burn out, or are burned; and the good ones are snatched up to be college or university presidents by the time you graduate from the place you picked five years ago. Faculty members themselves also move around a great deal more than before, and salary competition has even entered the ivy halls; who goes where and who lands whom is thought to be reflected in the measures of academic reputation and the sense of which law schools are "hot."

What doesn't change? Ask any broker. Ask Coldwell Banker.

Location. Location. Location.

According to the National Association for Law Placement's

> **Beyond the top schools: the first rule of targeting is location.**
>
> Chances are, you will practice law where you go to law school. Take out a map. Draw a big circle. That's where you're going to live. Friends for life.

most recent survey, 77 percent of jobs accepted by law graduates are in the same region where they went to law school. You know what this means: that's where you took the bar. That's where you're likely to stay. Your law school classmates are the ones you'll practice with, who'll recommend cases to you, serve as opposing counsel, judges later, etc. etc.

You don't just go to a law school. At its best, you join a law school network, a legal community, defined not simply by a Trojan or a Bruin or a crimson tide, but by a shared experience . . . and ethic.

Where do you want to live? Where do you want to work? All other things being equal, focus there. College is a great time to explore someplace where you've never been and live someplace where you may never return. Not necessarily for law school. Time to come home. Time to establish a reputation, make contacts, build a base. You're a grown-up now, or you're about to be.

AVERAGE STARTING SALARY BASED ON REGION

Data from Altman Weil as reprinted in the *National Jurist* (January 2002)

- **Pacific** ($66,150): Alaska, California, Hawaii, Oregon, and Washington
- **Mountain** ($63,333): Arizona, Colorado, Idaho, Montana, New Mexico, Nevada, Utah, and Wyoming
- **West South Central** ($71,365): Arkansas, Louisiana, Oklahoma, and Texas
- **East South Central** ($64,150): Alabama, Kentucky, Tennessee, and Mississippi
- **West North Central** ($64,000): Iowa, Kansas, Minnesota, Missouri, North Dakota, Oklahoma, and South Dakota
- **East North Central** ($73,111): Illinois, Indiana, Michigan, Ohio, and Wisconsin
- **South Atlantic** ($70,398): District of Columbia, Florida, Georgia, Maryland, North Carolina, South Carolina, Virginia, and West Virginia
- **Middle Atlantic** ($73,237): New Jersey, New York, Delaware, and Pennsylvania
- **New England** ($53,438): Connecticut, Maine, Massachusetts, New Hampshire, Rhode Island, and Vermont

2002 BAR PASSAGE RATES FOR ALL STATES

STATE	TOTAL EXAM TAKERS	PERCENT PASSING	STATE	TOTAL EXAM TAKERS	PERCENT PASSING
Alabama	909	55%	Montana	119	79%
Alaska	95	54%	Nebraska	192	76%
Arizona	990	70%	Nevada	599	59%
Arkansas	312	68%	New Hampshire	279	60%
California	11,581	45%	New Jersey	4,099	63%
Colorado	1,118	71%	New Mexico	275	86%
Connecticut	1,224	73%	New York	12,860	61%
Delaware	256	62%	North Carolina	1,067	66%
District of Columbia	647	55%	North Dakota	34	85%
Florida	3,573	68%	Ohio	1,746	65%
Georgia	1,452	70%	Oklahoma	439	69%
Hawaii	252	68%	Oregon	726	71%
Idaho	183	60%	Pennsylvania	2,647	65%
Illinois	3,451	72%	Rhode Island	224	57%
Indiana	761	70%	South Carolina	443	78%
Iowa	243	80%	South Dakota	74	93%
Kansas	524	82%	Tennessee	712	67%
Kentucky	477	76%	Texas	3,604	68%
Louisiana	804	67%	Utah	382	84%
Maine	285	62%	Vermont	107	71%
Maryland	2,063	61%	Virginia	1,878	64%
Massachusetts	2,789	66%	Washington	1,294	71%
Michigan	1,209	74%	West Virginia	314	64%
Minnesota	847	82%	Wisconsin	297	74%
Mississippi	396	81%	Wyoming	91	66%
Missouri	1,162	73%			

The Bar Examiner: National Conference of Bar Examiners, *2002 Statistics* (May 2003).

If you want to practice in Los Angeles, and the choice is USC versus Penn, I'd recommend USC. Same choice but you intend to practice in Philadelphia, go to Penn. As between Northwestern and Penn, if you want to practice in Chicago, go to Northwestern. If you want to practice in Philadelphia, Penn. If you want to practice in D.C. and you didn't get into Harvard, Yale, or Stanford, go to Georgetown over Northwestern or Penn.

If you want to practice in San Francisco, go to Berkeley over Michigan. If you want to practice in Detroit, do just the opposite. If you want to go to New York, go to NYU or Columbia over Berkeley or Michigan, unless you have a particular reason not to, in which case you will also be fine. If you want to go into government, go to Washington. If you get into Georgetown, go.

You don't need to check the ratings; you only need to check a map.

A national law school is a very good law school located in a place where law students don't want to live (did someone say Ann Arbor?).

Let me prove my point with the help of Professor Brian Leiter of Texas, the ratings guru of academics. He was looking at which schools are truly "national" in terms of job placement by evaluating the hiring practices of some of the nation's most selective law firms. He found sixteen law schools:

THE MOST NATIONAL LAW SCHOOL
BASED ON JOB PLACEMENT IN ELITE LAW FIRMS

RANK	SCHOOL	NORMALIZED SCORE	FACULTY QUALITY RANK (2003)	TEACHING QUALITY (2003)	STUDENT QUALITY RANK (2000)	PLACEMENT IN LAW TEACHING RANK (2002)
1	Harvard	100	2 (4.7)	Adequate	2	2–3
2	Chicago	88	2 (4.7)	Outstanding	4	4–5
3	Yale	86	1 (4.8)	Good	1	1
4	Virginia	82	10 (4.0)	Strong	7	6–8
5	Michigan	76	8 (4.1)	Adequate	9	4–5
6	Stanford	72	4 (4.5)	Adequate	4	2–3
7	Columbia	71	5 (4.3)	Adequate	7	6–8
8	Georgetown	69	12 (3.8)	Adequate	11	10–15
9	Duke	68	17 (3.5)	Adequate	13	10–15
10	Penn	66	11 (3.9)	Adequate	10	10–15
11	NYU	65	5 (4.3)	Adequate	3	9
12	Texas	56	8 (4.1)	Outstanding	16	10–15
13	Northwestern	53	14 (3.7)	Adequate	14	10–15
14	Vanderbilt	49	18 (3.4)	Strong	16	16–20
15	Cornell	47	14 (3.7)	Strong	14	10–15
16	Berkeley	45	7 (4.2)	Adequate	6	6–8
OTHER SCHOOLS STUDIED						
	George Washington	44	22 (3.1)	Adequate	29	21–50
	Minnesota	42	21 (3.2)	Adequate	18	16–20
	Notre Dame	37	Runner-up for top 40 (2.4)	Outstanding	27	21–50
	UCLA	35	14 (3.7)	Adequate	12	16–20
	Emory	33	29 (2.8)	Good	33	21–50
	Washington & Lee	26	32 (2.7)	Strong	23	21–50

Now you look at this list, and something should jump right out at you, or it does at me, anyway. There are a whole bunch of schools in the wrong place (and some aren't on the list at all). What is Columbia doing at seven, and NYU doing at eleven? How did Berkeley manage to finish behind Vanderbilt? This makes no sense, you might say.

But it makes perfect sense.

The way Professor Leiter determined "national" law schools, rightly so, was by looking at who sends their graduates to the top firms "nationally." Using numbers from "The Vault's" survey of associates, which ranks law firms, he looked at which schools were represented among the top three firms in each city/region. Berkeley finishes behind Vanderbilt because no one wants to leave California, and there are only six California firms on the list. I can't remember the last time I had a student who wanted a job in Cleveland or Detroit, and my guess is, the same is true at UCLA. That's why it's not on the list. It's why Michigan is above Stanford. Detroit doesn't hold that many of its graduates. Not so New York, vis-à-vis Columbia and NYU.

It doesn't matter that Yale may be ranked higher in *U.S. News*. Consider the law firm of Cravath, Swaine and Moore, considered by some to be the most selective firm in the country. More Cravath lawyers come from Harvard than from any other school. (See table on following page.) No surprise there. Harvard is the biggest school by far of the top three. But numbers two and three on the list are not Yale and Stanford: they are Columbia and NYU for Cravath. And number four? It's Fordham. That's correct. Fordham. A local school that's not on anybody's top ten list. Twenty-eight Cravath lawyers come from Fordham—more than from Yale. Now you have to graduate at the very top of your class at Fordham to get a job at Cravath, but it's doable.

HIRING BY SOME VERY SELECTIVE FIRMS

RANK	SCHOOL	NUMBER OF CRAVATH ATTORNEYS (NEW YORK OFFICE)
1	Harvard University	110
2	Columbia University	88
3	New York University	59
4	Fordham University	28
5	Yale University	24
6	University of Pennsylvania	19
7	Georgetown University	16
	University of Chicago	16
9	University of Texas, Austin	11
10	University of Virginia	9
11	Boston University	8
	Cornell University	8
13	Brooklyn Law School	7
14	University of California, Berkeley	5
15	Northwestern University	4
	University of Michigan	4
17	Duke University	3
	Rutgers University, Newark	3

At Wilmer, Cutler in D.C., Harvard is number one again, followed this time by Georgetown at number two, Yale at number three, and Duke at number four. George Washington ties with Stanford. At Los Angeles's O'Melveny & Myers, Harvard is again number one, tied with Loyola of Los Angeles (never heard of it, I bet, if you're not from L.A.), followed by UCLA, Berkeley, and USC. (See tables on following page.)

RANK	SCHOOL	NUMBER OF WILMER ATTORNEYS (WASHINGTON, DC OFFICE)
1	Harvard University	54
2	Georgetown University	31
3	Yale University	27
4	Duke University	18
5	University of Pennsylvania	15
	University of Virginia	15
7	University of Chicago	14
	University of Michigan	14
9	George Washington University	12
	Stanford University	12
11	Columbia University	11
12	American University	7
	New York University	7
	Vanderbilt University	7
15	University of Texas, Austin	6
16	Catholic University	4
	Cornell University	4
	University of North Carolina	4
19	Boston University	3
	Univ. of California, Berkeley	3
	University of Iowa	3

RANK	SCHOOL	NUMBER OF O'MELVENY ATTORNEYS (LOS ANGELES OFFICE)
1	Harvard University	32
	Loyola Law School, Los Angeles	32
3	University of California, Los Angeles	29
4	University of California, Berkeley	19
5	University of Southern California	17

RANK	SCHOOL	NUMBER OF O'MELVENY ATTORNEYS (LOS ANGELES OFFICE)
6	Yale University	14
7	Stanford University	13
8	Univ. of California, Hastings	10
9	Columbia University	7
	University of Virginia	7
11	University of Michigan	6
12	Georgetown University	5
	New York University	5
	Southwestern University	5
	University of Oregon	5
	University of Texas, Austin	5
17	George Washington University	4
	Pepperdine University	4
	University of Washington, Seattle	4
20	Cornell University	3
	Duke University	3
	Northwestern University	3
	University of Chicago	3

Now, there's a limit to this analysis. At Morrison and Forester in San Francisco, for instance, Berkeley, Hastings, and Stanford rank one, two, and three in terms of the number of attorneys. But local schools like Santa Clara and Golden Gate did not have as many attorneys practicing there as much better out-of-town schools like Duke, Minnesota, and Emory. (See table on following page.)

Obviously, if you get into a much better school out of town than you do in town, a T14 school out of town, and not in town, I would go there.

RANK	SCHOOL	NUMBER OF MORRISON ATTORNEYS (SAN FRANCISCO OFFICE)
1	Univ. of California, Berkeley	44
2	Univ. of California, Hastings	32
3	Stanford University	22
4	Harvard University	21
5	Yale University	18
6	Univ. of California, Los Angeles	15
7	New York University	11
8	University of Chicago	10
	University of Michigan	10
10	Cornell University	9
	Northwestern University	9
12	Columbia University	7
13	Georgetown University	6
	Univ. of California, Davis	6
15	University of Minnesota	5
16	University of Texas, Austin	4
	University of Virginia	4
18	Duke University	3
	Emory University	3
	McGeorge School of Law	3

In fact, if you really are flexible, you might consider a **two-pronged strategy**. Apply deep in the city where you want to live (see the city-by-city guide) and broadly in the places where they might just find you an exotic bird.

For every rule, there is a counterrule: What's common in your town is exotic out of town; a southerner in the Midwest looks different; a "Hollywood Producer" in Washington brings something different; a congressional staffer's cachet grows when she leaves Washington; accents sound better out of town.

The counterrule to the "local" rule is to find a place where you're considered exotic. If everyone else is using *U.S. News*, use a different ratings system. Find schools that are "underrated by *U.S. News* . . ." Find cities that you are willing to live in but that other people consider less desirable: the colder and more rural the city, the easier relative to its numbers that school or university will generally be for admission . . .

Careers in your lifetime will last longer, and take many more turns, than most of us can even imagine.

> ## *The more open you really are,*
> ## *the more choices you have.*

If staying local is a recipe for disappointment, by all means turn the rule on its head. Make yourself exotic and one of a kind; someone who brings a unique perspective because you're not one of them can get into a better law school out of town, somewhere different, than you ever could at home . . .

Does this work for everyone? Absolutely not. It's ideal for the 20 percent who aren't necessarily going to get their first

> If the first rule is location, the second rule is to pick the location where there are the fewest people like you.

job in the same state where they're going to school or who aren't necessarily going to become lawyers at all. . . .

Everyone I know in academics thinks that the best ratings—surprise, surprise—are done by an academic, based on surveys of, you guessed it, other academics, based on lists of who teaches where. Professor Leiter, some of whose other numbers I cited previously on the survey of "national" law schools, also does the "Educational Quality Rankings," in which he does the best job of anyone in explaining how the *U.S. News* rankings are done, what the problems are with their methodology, and why his is a more accurate measure of the quality of the education that you will receive. So what does he think? Or rather, what do we think? Here's what:

Professor Leiter's Educational Quality List:
(The academic's answer to *U.S. News* . . .)

RANK	SCHOOL (NUMBER OF FACULTY)	MEAN	MEDIAN
	THE TOP 40 LAW SCHOOLS BASED ON FACULTY QUALITY, 2003–2004		
1	Yale University (53)	4.8	5
2	Harvard University (80)	4.7	5
	University of Chicago (35)	4.7	5
4	Stanford University (40)	4.5	4.5
5	Columbia University (61)	4.3	4.5
	New York University (82)	4.3	4.5
7	University of California, Berkeley (54)	4.2	4.5
8	University of Michigan, Ann Arbor (52)	4.1	4
	University of Texas, Austin (73)	4.1	4
10	University of Virginia (60)	4	4
11	University of Pennsylvania (45)	3.9	4
12	Georgetown University (87)	3.8	4
	University of Southern California (43)	3.8	4

THE TOP 40 LAW SCHOOLS BASED ON FACULTY QUALITY, 2003–2004

RANK	SCHOOL (NUMBER OF FACULTY)	MEAN	MEDIAN
14	Cornell University (32)	3.7	3.75
	Northwestern University (50)	3.7	4
	University of California, Los Angeles (62)	3.7	4
17	Duke University (47)	3.5	3.5
18	Vanderbilt University (39)	3.4	3.5
19	Boston University (54)	3.3	3.5
	University of Iowa (40)	3.3	3.5
21	University of Minnesota, Twin Cities (49)	3.2	3
22	George Washington University (66)	3.1	3.25
	University of Illinois, Urbana–Champaign (35)	3.1	3
	University of San Diego (47)	3.1	3
	University of Wisconsin, Madison (49)	3.1	3
26	Fordham University (58)	3	3
	George Mason University (40)	3	3
28	Cardozo Law School/Yeshiva University (40)	2.9	3
29	Emory University (40)	2.8	2.75
	University of California, Hastings (51)	2.8	3
	Washington University, St. Louis (38)	2.8	3
32	Boston College (36)	2.7	2.5
	Ohio State University (44)	2.7	2.5
	University of California, Davis (27)	2.7	3
	University of North Carolina, Chapel Hill (46)	2.7	2.5
	Washington & Lee University (33)	2.7	3
37	Chicago-Kent College of Law (37)	2.6	2.5
	College of William & Mary (30)	2.6	2.5
	Rutgers University, Camden (39)	2.6	2.5
40	Arizona State University (35)	2.5	2.5
	Indiana University, Bloomington (40)	2.5	2.5
	Tulane University (45)	2.5	2.5
	University of Arizona (33)	2.5	2.5
	University of Colorado, Boulder (29)	2.5	2.5

(continued)

RANK	SCHOOL (NUMBER OF FACULTY)	MEAN	MEDIAN
\multicolumn{4}{c}{**THE TOP 40 LAW SCHOOLS BASED ON FACULTY QUALITY, 2003–2004**}			
	University of Miami (48)	2.5	2.5
	Runners–Up for the Top 40:		
	American University (51)	2.4	2.5
	Brooklyn Law School (43)	2.4	2.5
	Rutgers University, Newark (39)	2.4	2.5
	University of Florida, Gainesville (59)	2.4	2.5
	University of Notre Dame (37)	2.4	2.5

More rankings available at https://www.utexas.edu/law/faculty/bleiter/
rankings02/rankings.html.

UNDERRATED BY *U.S. NEWS*—SLEEPERS:

Even if you just compare *U.S. News* and Professor Leiter on the measure of academic reputation and faculty quality, you get some big discrepancies, as Professor Leiter himself points out:

Schools rated at least 40 percent higher by Professor Leiter than *U.S. News*. Let's call them, for fun, the sleepers (if you could ever call Chicago a sleeper):

1. University of Chicago (4th in *U.S. News*, 2nd in EQR)
2. University of San Diego (63rd in *U.S. News*, 22nd in EQR)
3. George Mason University (63rd in *U.S. News*, 26th in EQR)
4. Cardozo Law School/Yeshiva University (55th in *U.S. News*, 28th in EQR)
5. Rutgers University, Camden (71st in *U.S. News*, 37th in EQR)

Schools rated 25 percent higher by Professor Leiter than *U.S. News*:

1. New York University (8th in *U.S. News*, 5th in EQR)
2. University of Texas, Austin (12th in *U.S. News*, 8th in EQR)
3. University of Southern California (18th in *U.S. News*, 12th in EQR)
4. Boston University (25th in *U.S. News*, 19th in EQR)
5. Fordham University (36th in *U.S. News*, 26th in EQR)
6. Chicago-Kent College of Law (55th in *U.S. News*, 37th in EQR)

Schools rated 10 percent higher by Professor Leiter than *U.S. News:*

1. University of California, Los Angeles (16th in *U.S. News*, 14th in EQR)
2. George Washington University (25th in *U.S. News*, 22nd in EQR)
3. Arizona State University (51st in *U.S. News*, 40th in EQR)
4. University of Miami (44th in *U.S. News*, 40th in EQR)

Schools rated at least 50 percent lower by Professor Leiter than in the *U.S. News* **academic reputation survey include:**

1. Duke University (11th in *U.S. News*, 17th in this survey) (Professor Leiter's favorite overrated school)
2. University of Washington, Seattle (31st in *U.S. News*, not even a runner-up to the top forty in this survey)

Feeling better yet?

So you've come to grips with the fact that you can't get into Harvard and Yale. Or Columbia or NYU. Or USC or UCLA.

But can you get in anywhere?

Forget about location when your world has fallen apart. Okay. I've been there. Next list:

SUSAN'S SLEEPER SCHOOLS:

Schools that will impress Aunt Bea and that you can get into without a 165 . . .

or a 160 . . .

or a 4.0 . . .

or a 3.75 . . .

1. *Tulane Law School* (156–161; 3.2–3.6): I would've guessed higher . . . And if I would've guessed higher, anyone would. Maybe it's a throwback to the civil-law system, but as I said, you can learn what you want where you want and you can certainly have more fun some places than others. So you opened your envelope and it's a 157. Three years in New Orleans. Don't whine.

2. *University of Miami Law School* (153–158; 3.1–3.5): It has a first-rate faculty, a great president in Donna Shalala, and the advantage of being the "best law school" in a great, big city. Now here's the interesting part: the envelope, please: 153–158; 3.16–3.56. Not so tough. Fun city. Excellent weather. Really first-rate legal community, exciting practice if you stay there. So you got a 155 . . . this is a great school.

3. *Vermont Law School* (149–156; 2.8–3.3): Not far from Dartmouth College; established in 1972, with an emphasis

on environmental law. Did you see those numbers? In 2001, 781 applied and 515 were accepted; that's about as high an acceptance rate as you're going to see. They're trying to do something interesting. And what do you tell your friends? That you're going to New England . . . After all, everyone just assumes that if it's in New England, it's hard to get admitted.

4. *University of New Mexico* (151–160; 3.0–3.6): Good law school, strong clinical program, great city (Albuquerque), great place to live. In 2001, 650 applied and 251 were accepted; in-state tuition is under $6,000 at this writing.

5. *Case Western Reserve Law School* (155–160; 3.0–3.4): The best law school in Cleveland; okay, maybe Cleveland isn't your first-choice city; if it were, you might be happy that Case Western has been through the turmoil that it has at the university level, which might explain why the numbers aren't higher for the law school. In the meantime, Cleveland is a big city with a prestigious medical school and a reputation as a powerhouse in corporate America.

6. *Syracuse University* (148–154; 3.0–3.5): Okay, I know it's cold, but so is Cornell, and Syracuse is a lot easier to get into, and quite respectable. Joe Biden went there, and if you got a 150 or so, you could do a lot, lot worse, so buck up and go to work on that essay.

7. *University of the Pacific, McGeorge School of Law* (150–156; 2.8–3.3): In Sacramento; a top choice if you want to run state government in California. Its numbers for bar passage are much higher than the admission figures would suggest; with a new dean and a rising image, it's a comer . . .

8. *Catholic University of America College of Law* (154–158; 3.0–3.5): In Washington, D.C., see above. You can always claim a religious revival.

9. *Chicago Kent College of Law* (154–158; 3.0–3.5): Good school, better numbers . . .

10. *Suffolk Law School* (153–157; 2.9–3.4): *U.S. News* puts Suffolk in its "fourth tier" but that's certainly not what it feels like when you're there; Suffolk has a fabulous new building, located right in the heart of downtown Boston, a terrific faculty, great political connections in Massachusetts, and a top-notch clinical program.

COMING UP WITH YOUR OWN LIST OF NOMINEES

Ultimately, it's not rocket science:

You want to live in city X or state B. Apply to the top schools there. How far down the list do you go? What are your numbers?

Most people apply to a couple of reach schools, more than a couple in the middle, two that you're 99 percent certain you should get into. How many schools you apply to depends on your budget, tolerance for pain and rejection, indecision, etc.

Maybe you want to pick a few out-of-town schools that are reaches, but you think you have a shot. If you really are up in the air on where you would live or whether you might want to go abroad, then the regional argument is less powerful.

Maybe you have no geographic mobility, in which case there is simply no point in applying anywhere but in the city where you live and where there may be three schools in which you would enroll.

Be Realistic: One student with a 157 and a 3.4 came to me with a list that included every single top ten school. I asked him, nicely, if he was crazy. He pointed out, somewhat obnoxiously, that he had done the research and discovered that every one of those schools admitted at least one or two students each year with numbers like his. That's true. But none of them are privileged white kids who weren't Olympic athletes. He didn't listen. He got incredibly depressed after being rejected by every single top ten school about ninety seconds after they got his application. Want to throw money away and guarantee depression? Why?

It's one thing to put "reach" schools on your list. But don't set yourself up. You want to get into law school, not wallpaper your bathroom with rejection letters.

Apply Early: Don't wait until the last minute. I want to strangle students who walk into my office two days before recommendations are due and sheepishly hand me the forms. What do they think? Of course I'll do it—in twenty minutes. If it's not important enough to you to do in advance so as to give me time to do thoughtfully, well, you know what you get. . . .

But it's not just about recommendations. The longer you wait, the harder it is to get in. There seems to be no question about that. Virtually everybody rolls their admissions. Virtually every admissions person I talked to acknowledges that as time goes along, his or her standards get tougher. So what does that mean? Vote early, vote often, we used to say. Why make things more difficult than necessary? But I say that, over and over, and do people apply early? No. Bill Hoye tells me that at USC, for instance, we can get as many as half our applications in the last three weeks. Now everyone knows to apply early, and yet half the applicants don't. Why not?

Political Atmosphere: Does it matter to you that Chicago has a reputation for being conservative and more oriented toward "law and economics"? Yale, which used to be considered the "liberal" law school, is now closer to Chicago, while NYU is considered more liberal and public interest oriented. Harvard, which used to be considered the Beirut of legal education, has mostly settled down; the young turks have gotten old. But it's not warm and fuzzy; it's exciting and engaging at its best, cold, overwhelming and intimidating at its worst, and much of that depends on how you deal with it.

Physical Environment: The space you're in matters. For some people, it is critical. Yet knowing that, many people ignore entirely physical environment as an issue in choosing a law school.

Do you want/need/thrive on a campus? In a city? In a dorm? In an apartment? Some law schools have dorms, some don't. You're going to spend three years there. Whether you're somewhat happy or totally miserable in your environment will have more to do with how you do than what you think.

What kind of community are you looking for? Go visit, if you possibly can. This is useful for getting money, anyway. See below. Also, schools have different atmospheres. The atmosphere at Stanford really is different from Harvard. You're cheating yourself out of three years of your life if you don't check it out. Sit in on a class. Talk to students. There is a very good chance that you will end up living in the city/region where you go to law school, friends for life with the people you go to law school with.

This is a truly life-changing decision. It is worth the time to make it carefully.

By the time you graduate, the rankings will be different. Five years out, they'll be different. Ten years out, they'll be different. You'll still be in Cleveland. Get it?

Avoid Unaccredited Schools like the plague. There is a difference between "real" law schools awaiting accreditation (be careful) and matchbook law schools that will never be accredited. Don't waste money on the latter. Wait a year. Do something else. Their bar-passage rates are ridiculously low. Even those students who pass the bar rarely find jobs as lawyers. It's not the law school experience. They take people's money and don't turn out lawyers, don't teach you to think like a lawyer. Nothing. Their faculty tends to be awful. As for schools awaiting accreditation, get it in writing. Seriously. Otherwise you could end up suing, as a group of students here in California did recently after their school failed to become accredited as promised.

IS THERE A POINT AT WHICH IT'S NOT "WORTH IT" TO GO TO LAW SCHOOL, WHERE, IF YOU CAN'T GET INTO YOUR FIRST THREE OR FOUR CHOICES, YOU JUST SHOULDN'T GO?

The answer—guess what—is that it depends on why you're applying in the first place. There is very little point in going to Whittier or Western State if you want to end up only at O'Melveny and Myers or Gibson, Dunn and Crutcher, particularly if you want to get there right away. Or their equivalent in any other city in the country.

But the justice system in Orange County very clearly depends upon the graduates of Western State to administer it. Many of the poorest people in the county depend on the graduates of Western State to represent them in that system, as do the prosecutors' offices and city attorneys' offices.

Is it worth it?
Why are you going?

The further down you go in the rankings, the less likely you are to end up as a law professor, a partner in a large law firm, a law clerk, or a federal judge. Four out of nine of the current justices on the Supreme Court graduated from Harvard Law School and one more, Justice Ginsburg, spent a year there. Two more graduated from Stanford and one from Yale. I assure you that Justice Stevens, a Northwestern graduate, feels just fine about himself.

On the other hand, you don't have to go to Harvard to get elected to the Senate.

United States Senators Who Did Not Get Their Law Degrees at Harvard (or Yale or Stanford):

- Joe Biden, Syracuse (even on my easier-than-you-think list)

- Tom Harkin, Catholic University of America (ditto)
- Gordon Smith, Southwestern Law School
- Lisa Murkowski, Willamette College of Law
- Orrin Hatch, University of Pittsburgh
- Saxby Chambliss, University of Tennessee
- Pete Dominici, University of Denver Law School

The "local" rule is the one that holds truest for the Senate.

United States Senators Who Stayed Near Home to Go to Law School:

- Evan Bayh, Indiana University School of Law
- Sam Brownback, University of Kansas
- John Breaux, Louisiana State University
- John Cornyn, St. Mary's School of Law, Texas
- Lindsey Graham, University of South Carolina
- John Edwards, University of North Carolina

(continued)

- Mike DeWine, Northern Ohio University College of Law
- Saxby Chambliss, University of Tennessee
- Trent Lott, University of Mississippi
- Richard Shelby, University of Alabama School of Law
- George Voinovich, Ohio State University College of Law
- Jon Kyl, University of Arizona

Local Lawyers Who Have Done Just Fine, Thank You . . .

- Gloria Allred, sex discrimination attorney; Johnnie Cochran, attorney and television anchor; and Mark Geragos, criminal-defense lawyer; all went to Loyola Law School, Los Angeles.
- Marcia Clark, former O.J. prosecutor and television anchor, went to Southwestern.
- F. Lee Bailey, also on the Dream Team and even more famous in his time, went to Boston University.
- Okay, Alan Dershowitz went to Yale.

DEALING WITH REJECTION

David Burman, now a partner in Perkins, Coie, one of the top national law firms, clerked on the Supreme Court the same year I did, after he'd served as the editor in chief of the *Georgetown Law Journal*.

"Did you get rejected by any law schools?" I asked him.

"Yes," he replied. "Harvard (and a couple of others). Shortly after I started at Georgetown, one of your classmates sent me a clipping from the Harvard Law newspaper touting the fact that they had been able to find someone qualified for the entering class from every state except Wyoming (where I was from). It probably had something to do with motivating me during the remainder of law school."

Let it be an inspiration to you. Only one person can be first in the class at Harvard. Doing well at a regional school can get you just as far. Doing really really well can get you even farther. As I discovered in my little survey, many of the people I clerked with who didn't go to Harvard, Yale, or Stanford got rejected from those schools.

If you've done your best in the application process, targeted your applications, sparkled as bright as you can: **Go be a lawyer, and don't look back.**

{ 12 }

FINANCING YOUR
LEGAL EDUCATION

The cost of a legal education continues to increase. The average law student today graduates with $98,000 in debt.

15 MOST EXPENSIVE LAW SCHOOLS			
SCHOOL	RESIDENT FULL-TIME	NONRESIDENT FULL-TIME	RANKING
New York University	$33,503	$33,503	Next 3
Columbia University	$33,484	$33,484	Next 3
University of Southern California	$32,145	$32,145	Top 20
Northwestern University	$32,008	$32,008	Top 20
Yale University	$31,400	$31,400	Top 3
Cornell University	$31,250	$31,250	Top 10
Stanford University	$31,230	$31,230	Top 3
University of Chicago	$31,170	$31,170	Top 10
University of Pennsylvania	$31,138	$31,138	Top 10
Duke University	$30,556	$30,556	Top 20
Harvard University	$30,520	$30,520	Top 3

(continued)

15 MOST EXPENSIVE LAW SCHOOLS

SCHOOL	RESIDENT FULL-TIME	NONRESIDENT FULL-TIME	RANKING
Fordham University	$29,946	$29,946	Top 40
Georgetown University	$29,440	$29,440	Top 20
George Washington University	$29,420	$29,420	Top 30
Yeshiva University (Cardozo School of Law)	$29,200	$29,200	Top 60

15 MOST INEXPENSIVE LAW SCHOOLS (BY RESIDENT TUITION)

SCHOOL	RESIDENT FULL-TIME	NONRESIDENT FULL-TIME	RANKING
North Carolina Central University	$3,375	$14,753	Tier 4
Southern University	$3,782	$8,382	Tier 4
Georgia State University	$4,470	$15,558	Top 100
University of North Dakota	$4,826	$10,624	Tier 3
University of Wyoming	$5,199	$10,863	Tier 3
University of Florida	$5,613	$19,863	Top 50
University of Nebraska	$5,760	$13,075	Top 70
Florida State University	$5,783	$20,664	Top 70
University of Georgia	$5,832	$20,850	Top 40
Arizona State University	$5,835	$14,355	Top 60
University of Arizona	$5,843	$14,363	Top 50
University of Idaho	$5,984	$12,704	Tier 3
University of New Mexico	$6,098	$18,559	Top 70
University of Alabama	$6,144	$12,850	Top 50
University of South Dakota	$6,160	$12,491	Tier 3

See Law School Admission Council, *Official Guide to ABA-Approved Law Schools* (visited February 13, 2004), available at http://officialguide.lsac.org/docs/cgi-bin/home.asp (Search by "All Law Schools" and "Tuition") (figures represent tuition for the 2003–2004 school year).

There is money available if you have done well. Schools will compete against one another. They will pay students with high numbers to attend. If you are one of those students, know your value.

DO NOT BE PENNY-WISE AND POUND-FOOLISH.

Okay. Easy for me to say now. I know what it's like not to have a dime, not to have anyone helping you, to have to work your first year when you're not supposed to. I used to fall asleep in class because I tended bar until one in the morning. The other reason I went to Harvard was because it was the cheapest law school I got into. I was a tenured professor at Harvard before I paid off my last loan. And law school was a whole lot cheaper then.

But if you get into your first-choice school, don't turn it down so fast because of money. You can make a lot of money as a lawyer. You can pay off the loans later.

The dirty little secret is that more and more scholarship money is going to "buy" top students rather than to help needy ones. Blame the ratings game. So what happens is that everybody talks about need and all that, but you find that your top choice schools may give you nothing, and your bottom-choice schools offer the world, and your parents look at you as if to say, "We've already paid for four years of college, isn't X school good enough?"

Maybe. Maybe not. Consider the choice this young woman made:

I was accepted at all the law schools I applied to, which included UCLA, Loyola L.A., Lewis & Clark . . . I chose my law school for several reasons. First, I received a full scholarship and was not prepared to waste that opportunity. Second, I chose based upon my "fit" within the school. Chapman is a young law school, filled with an entrepreneurial spirit I did not find at more established institutions. Finally, I was intrigued by attending a school where I could forge my own path and where the program and extracurriculars are still developing. I have immensely enjoyed law school, something I did not anticipate. I have not regretted my choice.

—RACHEL P., 3L;
Chapman University
School of Law

They're trying hard at Chapman. Buying good students. But there are certain doors open to UCLA grads that you have to spend a lot of time and energy opening yourself if you go to Chapman.

Say Rachel decides she wants to work for a big firm, wants to teach, wants to do sophisticated public-interest-law cases, wants to work at the U.S. attorney's office, wants to clerk on the federal bench . . . Will she regret her choice? Yes. Will doors be closed? Yes.

I am very happy with the law school I chose, and I had a hard decision to make—UConn vs. UPenn. While I'd prefer to live in a more vibrant city or area, I value the quality of life and the student body here . . . If I had to choose another law school to attend, it probably would have been UVA because I think the quality of life there is similar and they have a much stronger national reputation.

—H.D.M., 2L;
University of Connecticut
Law School

UConn is a very good law school. But going to Penn is a no-brainer, especially if the alternative is Virginia.

Understand what's going on. **I was horrified when I read responses like these and saw students say that they attended barely accredited law schools** (for instance, Chapman) **over top ten ones because of money.** No one will ever believe them. If they change their minds, and want to go into law teaching, or move across the country and work in a different city, or work for an elite law firm, doors will just be closed. The difference in salary expectations is, quite frankly, huge. It's one thing to choose USC over Stanford because we're paying the full bill and guaranteeing a summer job at Skadden (which we do for Frank Rothman Scholars). You're set. Fine. It's quite another to pick Chapman, which was accredited twenty minutes ago, over UCLA . . . Say it ain't so, Joe.

DO NOTHING TO HARM YOUR CREDIT RATING BEFORE LAW SCHOOL. CLEAN UP OLD DELINQUENCIES AND DEFAULTS.

Seventy-five percent of all law students borrow to get through law school.

You can't borrow from anybody if you destroy your credit rating before you get to law school.

- If you're delinquent (behind) on bills, pay up.
- If you've defaulted (never paid), pay back.
- Do not even think of declaring bankruptcy.

In the UConn example above, I'd tell the student who'd been admitted to Penn to go see the financial-aid people there and ask for help and advice. Remember that what sounds like a fortune now won't be a fortune later. My students, some of them, are starting at about $140,000 a year. You read that right. Live like a student for one more year and you pay off a big chunk of those loans. Go to Chapman and you're not going to get that job. Sorry but true. No one will believe you turned down Penn. Or they'll think, "Why would we hire someone with such poor judgment?"

AVERAGE AMOUNT OF FINANCIAL AID FOR FULL-TIME PROFESSIONAL STUDENTS BY SOURCE OF AID AND STUDENT CHARACTERISTICS

CHARACTERISTICS	ANY AID	FEDERAL AID	INSTITUTIONAL AID	OTHER
Total Grad Students	$22,803	$18,014	$7,456	$9,070
Law Students	$24,054	$17,201	$7,043	$11,637

PERCENTAGE OF ALL GRADUATE STUDENTS WHO RECEIVE FINANCIAL AID

Federal Aid	30% of all students
Institutional Aid	27% of all students
State Aid	3% of all students
Students with Loans	30% of all students
Total Aided Students	60% of all students

AVERAGE AID RATIOS FOR AIDED LAW STUDENTS (1999–2000)

Ratio of Federal Aid to Total Aid	78.0
Ratio of Institutional Aid to Total Aid	30.7
Ratio of Grants to Total Aid	30.7
Ratio of Loans to Total Aid	88.8

AVERAGE EXPENSES OF LAW STUDENTS (1999–2000)

FULL-TIME FULL-YEAR STUDENTS	
Total Student Budget	$31,128
Tuition and Fees	$16,468
Total Nontuition Expenses	$13,427
PART-TIME FULL-YEAR STUDENTS	
Tuition and Fees	$9,634

PERCENTAGE OF LAW STUDENTS WITH STAFFORD LOANS AND AVERAGE AMOUNTS

	TOTAL STAFFORD LOANS	SUBSIDIZED LOANS	UNSUBSIDIZED LOANS
Percent	82.3%	81%	74.5%
Average Amount	$16,447	$8,178	$9,285

AVERAGE AMOUNT BORROWED BY GRADUATE SCHOOL STUDENTS THROUGHOUT SCHOOL (PUBLIC VS. PRIVATE SCHOOLS)

	FIRST YEAR	SECOND YEAR	THIRD YEAR	TOTAL
Total	$36,321	$54,484	$70,691	$58,438
Public School	$27,332	$45,685	$62,960	$49,845
Private School	$42,857	$61,756	$76,215	$65,294

PERCENTAGE DISTRIBUTION OF LAW STUDENTS ACCORDING TO TIME BETWEEN RECEIVING BACHELOR'S DEGREE AND BEGINNING LAW SCHOOL (1999–2000)	
Less Than One Year	31.8
One–Two Years	35.8
Three–Six Years	19.5
Seven Years or More	12.9

U.S. Dept. of Education, National Center for Education Statistics, *1999–2000 National Postsecondary Student Aid Study* (2000), data available at http://nces.ed.gov/ViewRequests.asp?order=title.

PLAY SCHOOLS AGAINST ONE ANOTHER.

More schools than would like to admit it play. You didn't know this did you? Neither did I, until I started researching this book. I can't say I was entirely happy about what I learned.

This is another dirty little secret. Schools compete for students who will bring up their ratings—for students with the kind of numbers that raise the numbers of the schools, that in turn bring them better applicants, that in turn bring them more money from their provosts, etc.

How do they compete? They compete with **money** and **summer-job offers.** Before you start. That's right. Before you've even begun. Say you're trying to decide between three schools that have accepted you. Say money matters. Why wouldn't it? Say having a summer job to look forward to matters. Why wouldn't it? Say you have very good numbers, relative to the school, and a very nice smile. **Go to the accepted students' day.** Make an appointment to see the director of admissions and, if possible, the dean. Did you read that right? You did. The dean. Of the law school. Here's where you start to play. Pick the school that gave you the best package (not necessarily one of your top three). Consider that your minimum. Put it on the table. Tell whomever you're talking to that you'd much rather go to their school than that other school—if only they could match the package, provide the summer job, up the ante. And then watch the ball roll. Tell them how much better you like their school than that other school, were it not for the financial package that you'd been offered by that other school. Smile a lot.

Would it ever have occurred to me to do this when I was a senior in college? To be honest, no. But here's the truth: It works. I have talked to any number of students who did it, and have thousands and thousands of dollars in extra aid to show for it.

I know one student who told me that he had literally auctioned himself off among three fine law schools. I assumed he had a 179 and a 3.9. Nope. Not even close. He had a very good record, but not that good. As a matter of fact, not even close. High 160s, and that was the second time around . . . 3.6 . . . Wait-listed at Harvard. And he had schools bidding for him. Why? Because once he had them competing, they didn't want to lose. That's the other point. These guys are competitive. Once they get into the game, they want to win. This world is small enough that if you can get on the radar screen, you can become a hot property just because somebody else wants you. "What did you have that they wanted so badly?" I asked him.

"A nice smile," he said . . .

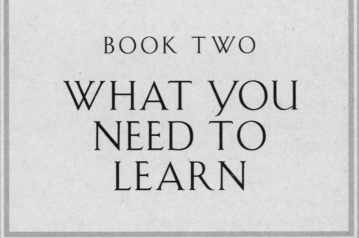

BOOK TWO

WHAT YOU
NEED TO
LEARN

CONGRATULATIONS

You made it. You're here. And whether or not this was your first-choice school last spring, there's about a 95 percent chance it's going to be your alma mater, so buy your hat or your sweatshirt or your bumper sticker, and get some school spirit, and get ready to work your tail off.

The good news is things aren't nearly as bad as they used to be. If you want to know what it used to be like, go see *The Paper Chase*. Read *1L*. That stuff really happened. The Kingsfields—the caricatured professors who lent you change to call your mother—have mostly returned. Too bad, in a way, because they were almost fun. Almost.

Nobody succeeds without really trying. But plenty of people really try, and don't succeed.

HERE'S THE BAD NEWS, UP FRONT

Law school is full of people like you. Overachievers. Basic hard workers. Good students. Turns out that isn't necessarily enough. Half the class ends up in the bottom half of the class for the first time in their lives.

What's worse, grades matter. How much they matter depends inversely on how fancy the law school is: the fancier it is, the less they matter; but the fancier it is, the more competitive the people tend to be, so try telling a bunch of Harvard 1Ls to chill. I taught there for ten years. "Chill" is not in the vocabulary. And even there, frankly, grades matter.

So congratulations, you're in. But who's got time to celebrate? You show up, and your roommate has already been to boot camp and decided where he wants to work. Professor Lawrence Krieger, in a recent article, describes consistently asking first-year law students what percent expected to finish in the top 10 percent of their class and finding that 90 percent answered that they did—meaning that about 80 percent, or more, are going to be disappointed.

What distinguishes the few who succeed, from the majority who don't? Then again, what's success? For every question, there's another question. Have you learned how to brief a case yet?

Probably the best advice I had was: "Do the best you can with what you have."

You asked if I ever had a job I hated. The answer is no. I felt lucky to have any job at all because no California firm was hiring women lawyers in *1952* when I graduated. I would happily have taken any position, whatever it was. I found that I had to take some jobs that initially were not promising and I tried with each of them to make something better out of the position.

If I had to do it all over again I would indeed go to law school. I thought the intellectual training provided in law school was splendid and my life has been shaped as a result of going to law school.

If I were going into private practice today, I would be interested in pursuing either intellectual property law or employment law.

As far as advice to young lawyers or law students today, I always suggest that the best thing to do is to learn to read fast and to write well.

—ASSOCIATE JUSTICE SANDRA DAY O'CONNOR,

U.S. Supreme Court

{ 13 }

WHAT YOU NEED TO KNOW BEFORE YOU BEGIN

It's simple. Brief cases. Don't brief cases. Outline. Don't outline. Start now. Wait. Go to classes. Don't go to classes. Grades. Grades. Not grades. Welcome to law school.

> *There are at least two answers to every question, and no guarantee that either will be right. The good news is that it used to be a whole lot worse.*

If you've seen *The Paper Chase*, or read *1L*, I can only say, it's just not that bad anymore. Was it ever that bad? Yes.

This is what one student wrote, and I think it sort of sums things up:

I started law school a bit blindly. I had heard about the Socratic method, but as far as learning or preparing for what the daily curriculum would entail, I was completely clueless.

A friend of mine had taken one of those "law school before law school" courses and seemed to already be stressing out the summer before first semester. I, on the other hand, was looking forward to embarking on an entirely new educational experience. In a strange sense, I wanted to be surprised.

And surprised I was. The first week of law school was unlike any other week of school I've gone through. Perhaps a course could have told me the workload would be rigorous, but anyone who has applied to law school already knows that. What can't be communicated is the feeling of full, immediate, and intense immersion demanded of you the second you walk in those law school doors. I was taken aback by the constant pressure in class to be attentive and prepared. Combine this with having to keep up with the long daily reading assignments . . . It becomes almost medieval. It's a rite of passage that can only be truly understood by experiencing it for real yourself. What else can I say? It's intense.

—MARK BERNS, 2L;
USC

In the old days, in the welcoming speeches, the dean would say, "Look to your left. Look to your right. One of those people won't be there at the end of the year." That's not true anymore. Everyone graduates. Dropout rates are minuscule. Maybe it's because we get better students. Maybe it's because of grade inflation. In either event, the danger is not failing, but failing to meet the standards you've set for yourself.

It's easy to get depressed before you begin. "Women don't do very well at Harvard," one of my first-year professors said to me at the opening-day picnic. Thanks a lot. **Beware of people who tell you that you're not going to do very well,** that you're not welcome on campus, that women/blacks/older students/Hispanics/etc. don't do very well, or that the school is second rate, or that you are . . . Believe them and it can become true.

The truth is that women didn't do very well at Harvard Law School, in part because they didn't get called on as much; there weren't any, and I mean *any*, female professors; there weren't many female students; and there wasn't any support (say, doctors in the health services who would take care of you if you had a gynecological problem, that sort of thing).

For some reason, there are always going to be first-year loudmouths, including sometimes professors, who can make you feel two inches tall, people who come in knowing the names of the fancy law firms, when you don't know any of them, know how to "brief" cases when you still think briefs are underwear, insist that they do all the talking, etc. Just re-member that these loudmouths tend to make up in volume for what they lack in gray matter.

Consider my experience with Jason Cord (not his real name, although at the time I thought it was), my first year moot-court partner. We were assigned to work together. He was one of those very large, heavyset, loudmouthed guys, a joint, JD/MBA student. We divided the brief in half. When it came time to do the oral argument, he divided the case in half, giving me one third, and himself two thirds. When it came to the reply, he told me to sit down, and he'd do the talking. I gave him notes, which he didn't even bother to look at. We lost. He said my section had been weak. He made me feel like a total failure. This was fairly early in the first semester of first year.

About a month later, there was a huge story in the *Boston Globe* about a guy who had managed to get into both law school and business school without ever graduating from college by submitting a totally phony application, complete with phony recommendations, etc. The joke was that he should be kicked out of law school and get his business degree early. He'd even made up a name. You guessed it. Jason Cord. And I let him tell me to shut up. It should go without saying that you don't want to be one of these loudmouths. Reputations made here count.

People start becoming their permanent selves in law school. Up to then, you're still kids. This is when the grown-up you starts. Stand around with a bunch of your parents' friends, and if a few of them are lawyers, the stories usually start in law school. When you start working, you'll notice that, too. Associations start getting made in law school; people will say, oh, we went to law school together, or he was a class ahead, or he's been like that since law school. Good and bad. So be generous of spirit. Lending someone your notes costs you nothing. The truth is that you learn by taking the notes, by figuring out what to write down, thinking it through, not just copying it over.

The guy sitting next to you asking for your notes could be on the state supreme court someday, deciding your client's future. Or he could have a major case to refer, and why not give it to the smartest guy in his law school class? *If* he remembers how nice that guy always was about sharing his notes.

YOU DON'T NEED TO GO TO PRE-LAW "BOOT CAMP."

You arrive and discover that everyone around you has taken classes "to get ready" for law school. They all know how to brief already.

Are you hopelessly behind the curve? Have your parents failed you already? The short answer is: no. The good news and bad news of law school is that your whole grade in every course is based on one exam that is a long time away, by which time any advantage conferred by boot camp will be long gone. Now you can let out your breath.

There is no end of innovations that people in the business

But if you're desperate to go anyway . . .

Princeton Review offers courses in eleven cities, which I was surprised to discover are taught by a number of my colleagues.

For information: www.lawpreview.com; price ranges from $1,075–$1,275 depending on when you register.

Advantage Education offers a weeklong program at the University of Michigan for $1,095.

For information: http//study-smart.com.

of "preparing" you for law school boards, tests, applications, etc. will come up with. Boot camp? I said, when I first heard about it. Do you lose weight? I asked. Get in shape? Is it the law school professors' full-employment act? For people who can't get enough of teaching LSAT prep courses, bar prep courses, one more chance to pay their own kids' tuition? Yes.

First, no one, repeat *no one*, "needs" to go. No law school in America expects its students to go to one of these places. They were created with one purpose: to make money for the people who created them, by feeding off the endless insecurity of people like you.

Go to the beach instead. Read a great book. Or a trashy book. Or go to Europe—or someplace you've never been. Do something wonderful that you'll never do again. Or work an extra week so you'll be that much less in debt.

Will boot camp harm you? No. Not unless whoever is teaching it is a total doofus who so completely turns you off to the law that you decide not to go to law school at all. At the big boot camps, they've actually got some big-name professors who are sure to amuse you and entertain you, and teach you a thing or two: for $1,000 or more, you should at least get that; who knows, maybe I'll see you there next year with my kids.

Can it help you? Sure. If you've been out of school for a while, and you're feeling rusty about your skills, about being back in a classroom, getting into the student thing, and you've got money to spare, why not? If you're ready to leave home early, your parents insist on an educational destination, why not? You're from a foreign country and are nervous about your command of English, why not? You've got some special circumstance, a disability, you're unusually nervous, require reassurance, you want to be an extra 1000 percent sure that you know how to brief a case before you get there . . .

But be realistic. Will it guarantee that you make *Law Review*, get better first-year grades, etc? Of course not. Whatever you get in that week, everybody else can get in their first week or month . . . Your first-year grades depend on one exam in each course, which doesn't come until December. Life is not fair.

> People who write well have the real head start. People who write fast have a head start. As in quickly, so they say more, write longer legible, better answers in less time.

People who write clearly, and I mean clearly as in neat penmanship, have a head start. Neater is better. If you don't know how to type yet, learn. Most law schools are moving toward allowing students to type exams. If you don't think professors appreciate a typed exam, well imagine reading seventy-five or a hundred! Besides, I have found my ability to sit down and bat something out, as in type faster than anyone else in the room, to be one of those skills that unlike my coffeemaking ability is a positive vestige of a sexist past. I doubt boot camp teaches touch typing, but it should.

One of the most important lessons of law school, as in life, is to change what you can, accept what you can't, decide what matters, and pick your fights.

GIVE YOURSELF THE TIME AND RESOURCES YOU NEED TO SUCCEED.

You're not supposed to have a job your first year. I did anyway. I had no choice. I needed the money. I liked eating. My roommate sold blood. I fell asleep the next morning after bartending the night before. It worked out okay, but it was hard on me.

If you have to work, you have to work. Bartend weekends. Babysit nights. Work at the library, where you can read. Do what you have to do. Barney Frank was a classmate of mine, and he was in the state legislature while he was going to law school. He turned down *Law Review.* He's in Congress now. He has had one heart attack, however. Lest you think I make it look easy. Nothing is ever as easy as it looks. Barney's slogan was: "Neatness isn't everything."

If you have a choice, it is better to go into debt. Better to wait until next year. Show your parents this page. It is really, really difficult. Even if you worked your way through college.

Law school is not the same. Especially first year. Law school eats time. Especially the legal methods stuff. It is like learning a new language. I can read a forty-page case in ten minutes. It will take you two hours. You have to read a case at least twice to be ready for class. Three times is ideal. Whether or not you brief. That's just the way it is. All things in due course, as they say. Doing better now will make you more money later.

> Do not work during the first year. No matter how financially strapped you are, good first-year grades will do more to help you pay off debt in the long run.
>
> —DAN WENNOGLE, 3L;
> *University of Denver*

Dan Wennogle's right.

There are some fine law schools that have nighttime/part-time programs. Most "top" law schools only have full-time programs. Besides, working full-time and going to law school nights is unbelievably difficult. Don't do it unless you have to and only for as long as you have to. **There is nothing redeeming about martyrdom.** Yes, it helps you keep your perspective. But you don't have to be sleep-deprived to do that. If there is no other way for you to become a lawyer, okay. But if you can wait a year and go full-time, wait. If you can take out a loan and go full-time, take out a loan. If you can beg your parents and go full-time, beg. Pride? What's that?

*I was an evening student working full-time my first year. Don't do it.
Don't do it. I have yet to see a full-time working evening student who
has breezed through it, or even managed to do work AND school sat-
isfactorily. I have since transferred to day, quit my job, and love life. I
am relatively poor, but resigned to having loans, and my low-cost school
keeps the expenses in control. You cannot have the best of both worlds;
there just aren't enough hours in the days. I received one lukewarm
warning, but I wish someone had emphatically told me it couldn't be
done (while staying sane) before I tried. If you must, however, work
full-time: I found that other similarly situated students were the most
supportive and sharing. There was NO competition, but a collegial
atmosphere where, if you missed a class, someone had notes for you the
next day. No one tells you about the good side of law students, and
that is a mistake.*

—NANCY KENNEDY, '04,
University of Connecticut
School of Law

I've been reading survival guides. One of them tells you to
go right out and buy the *Nutshell* and *Gilbert's*. I taught criminal law for seventeen years. The *Nutshell* and *Gilbert's* won't do
you any good at all in my course. I hate them. Useless if you
have me. The *LaFave Hornbook,* on the other hand, is my bible.
The problem is, it costs a bloody fortune. So every year I put a
bunch of copies on reserve in the library. I also encourage students to buy used ones from old students. Not much changes
in substantive criminal law. Murder is still murder. Even a very
old copy will do you much better than a new *Gilbert's*. As for
outlines, I personally prefer *Emmanuel's*. On the other hand, I
know some professors who hate *Emmanuel's*. You have to ask.
In other words, you don't know until you get there and see
whom you have.

It isn't contracts; it's contracts with Professor Whoever. Criminal procedure with Professor Whitebread. Criminal law with Professor Estrich.

The best person to ask about outlines/hornbooks/etc. is the professor him/herself. The second-best person is someone who did really well the year before. The worst person to ask is someone who wrote a generic book about surviving in law school and has no idea whom you're taking a class from, or what casebook you're using, or what approach your particular professor is taking, or what their "shtick" is . . . Any book that tells you to buy a particular handbook in advance is wrong. But wait. Let me guess. That book was published by the same company that publishes the guidebook they want you to buy? I don't want to know.

Don't buy used casebooks unless you really really have to. It's okay second and third year. I bought all used books second and third year. But the danger with buying used books during your first year is that you'll rely on someone else's underlines or highlights instead of doing your own. It's only human. When you're racing along, and it's late at night, who can help it? And the person who read it before you didn't know any more when he underlined than you do, and just may have underlined the wrong things . . . meaning you may miss what really matters. So try to buy a fresh copy. You can buy a used hornbook or a used outline if you need to. But not a used casebook.

{ 14 }

TO BRIEF OR NOT
TO BRIEF? THAT IS
THE QUESTION

In your first year, you take contracts, torts, and criminal law. But you don't really learn them. That's the weird part of first year. You think you're going to learn "the law." You think there is something called "the law." Then you get to law school, you get your books, and there's no law there. The better the law school, the less law you learn. I remember one of my first-year professors misstating the facts of a case. One of the smart boys raised his hand to "correct" him. "Oh," said the professor, "the facts don't matter." He was right, of course, but we were aghast. How could the facts not matter? Neither did the case. Except in constitutional law, the choice of cases is entirely haphazard. They're just there to prove a point—or rather, the lack of one. There is no ball. That's the ball they're hiding. And you thought that was "est."

Your first year is an introduction to common law, the way judges decide cases by applying judge-made law to facts. You learn some legislative "rules"—the rules of the Uniform

The First-Year Curriculum

Torts
- Injuries, wrongful acts.
- May be intentional or negligent or strict liability.
- Standards of liability and defenses.
- From train wrecks to car accidents to mass torts . . .
- Lots of economics.

Contracts
- Offer, Acceptance, Consideration, and Breach.
- How you measure damages.
- The Uniform Commerical Code.
- When contracts are and aren't implied and enforced, etc.

Civil Procedure
- How to sue: complaints, discovery, motions, and pleadings.
- The rules, and the values they serve.

Criminal Law
- If a dead man is shot in the desert, who is responsible for his death?

- If you have sex with an unconscious
  woman, can you claim you thought she was
  auditioning to be a porn star?

Constitutional Law
- What no one gets to practice, but everyone
  loves. Spoils you for life . . . not every
  school lets you taste it in the first year.
- With reason.

Legal Methods
- Here's the rub: learning to write, to research,
  to argue, is really important. But in most law
  schools, legal-methods instructors are second-
  class citizens, or students, who aren't trusted to
  give you real grades. So legal methods takes an
  enormous amount of time, but the payoff in
  terms of a grade is zero. Just warning you.

Commercial Code, for instance, a little criminal law, and some
civil procedure, but mostly you learn how the seemingly clear
and straightforward rules can almost always be manipulated by
clever lawyers (and professors): for every rule, there is a counterrule, or an exception, or you wouldn't be studying it.

In every case, you have facts, that give rise to issues. The issues are resolved by applying rules of general application. Like
cases are supposed to be decided alike. Results should be fore-
seeable in order to create certainty, and to make the law seem

fair and to make people accept the results. That's what it means to have a system of law, not of men. Of course we know men (and an occasional woman) made the law in the first place. They also have to make decisions in applying it. The cases in the book are chosen for the points they illustrate. Usually, they are there both as statements of particular black-letter rules, and as illustrative examples of the areas of uncertainty those rules typically create.

• Most of the time, you'll have one case holding one thing, and another case, that's almost the same, holding precisely the opposite, and you're supposed to figure out what makes them different, and if that's what really explains the different result. Then you have a bunch of questions afterward exploring possible theories. None of this has anything remotely to do with the law of the state you live in.

You're sitting in one state in 2004 reading a Pennsylvania decision from 1958. Why? Because it's a good explanation of foreseeability by a smart judge, and the guys who put together this casebook were looking for a foreseeability case. If you knew the point the case was there to make, you could be smarter about paying attention to the important things in reading it. You can be smarter by looking at the syllabus, the table of contents, and the questions at the back of the section before you start reading the cases. You could practically figure out a course's outline by doing that before the semester began, though you really wouldn't want to; it does spoil the fun. You need to believe, and let it build one piece at a time, understanding that what you're building is not an edifice but a process, a way of thinking more than a structure of thought.

The woman was driving a Ford Mustang. Does it matter

that it's a Mustang? Or that she was driving? It depends what the case is about—is it a lawsuit against Ford for defective gas tanks in the Mustang, or a prosecution of her husband for murder because he caught sight of her rendezvousing with another man after he recognized her car? Are the facts at issue here, or is the real issue whether that counts as provocation?

You read the case to find out not only what the court decided, but how it justified its result: what its reasoning was, its analysis, how it dealt with the arguments on the other side; then you read another case, that may come to an opposite conclusion, or demonstrate the problems with the approach, or why it's not been followed; or what happens when it's taken to its extreme; or what the opposite rule is; say what happens to a woman when she sees her husband in similar circumstances; or a case where the man has a day to think about it (if this is a chapter about cooling-off periods and provocation); or a case about the first Mustang gas tank to explode as opposed to the four-hundredth, and what difference it makes.

At the beginning, it takes you forever to read a three-page case because you don't know what to look for, what's important and what isn't, so everyone tells you to go through this elaborate process of briefing the case.

DO YOU NEED TO BRIEF?

Yes, but don't make a federal case of it. It will help you prepare for class. It will not help you prepare for the exam, at least not directly, which many students find bitterly disappointing after having invested enormous resources, financial (colored pens, etc.) and emotional, in briefing.

Briefing is a short-term investment. Advice books spend pages turning the briefing of cases into an art form. Boot camps do the same thing. They give you models, and super-models. The biggest single contributor to time wasted during the first year is not time spent going to class, but time spent briefing cases.

It is not an art form. You can look at the syllabus, and it will tell you right there what concepts you're supposed to be "getting." Go to the back—to the end of the section. Skim the questions. Now skim the case. Now go back and read it slowly and you should know as you do this just what you're looking for and why. Whether it's worth writing down in the facts that she was driving a Mustang or not . . . What the issue is. What the key to the holding is. What the case is about. Why it's there.

Once you get good at it, you can do it much faster. Once you get really good at it, you stop doing it, and never do it again. Briefing, I mean. Not reading cases. Good lawyers always read the cases themselves, always, because it's by reading the cases that you see things and think of things. But briefing? No. Take notes. Underline. Prepare to get called on in class. But don't make a federal case of it. Stop sooner rather than later, and spend the time reviewing what happened instead.

Don't get me wrong. There's nothing bad about briefing. Some people brief every case forever. They do an excellent job. Then they get mad because there is no direct relationship between briefing cases and doing well on exams, or even knowing the answers to follow-up questions in class. Sorry. There isn't. Briefing is just one way of getting material down, sifting through it, figuring out what the issues are, what the relevant facts are, how to apply issues to facts, etc.

Briefing is a discipline—a way of forcing yourself to do the reading instead of watching TV; something to look at in class when you get called on the first few times.

The key little secret is that at the end, **with the excep-**

tion of constitutional law, cases don't matter, so the facts of them don't matter, so how they got decided doesn't matter, so all the actual briefing is a complete waste of the paper it's written on.

In that sense, once you've fallen behind and know what you're supposed to know from the case, there is simply no point in going back and briefing it. The point is just to go back and figure out what you were supposed to have learned from it, and learn it and keep moving . . . Since I was always behind, I almost never briefed. And yes, it worked for me. But do I recommend it? No.

But know before you get too far that you will never look back on your briefs for the facts or the holding or any of that . . . **that their half-life is about a day** . . . and don't make writing them an art form, **make it a shorthand,** a way of focusing your analysis, a means and not an end in itself . . . because that's all briefs are.

{ 15 }

SURVIVING THE
SOCRATIC METHOD

When I was a first-year student, a classmate of mine "passed" in property law. As in, said "Pass"—when asked a question. No answer. There was a long silence. "Two no trump," Professor A. James Casner, then the dean of American property law, responded. There was another long silence. Then the student attempted to answer the question. No one ever passed again.

When I started teaching, one of my senior colleagues at Harvard explained to me how he prepared to teach a class. He had the world's most complicated decision tree, leading from the first question he asked, to every possible answer to that question, to every possible question he could ask based on every possible answer, to every possible follow-up question and answer, to every possible follow-up question and answer—all inevitably leading to the point he wanted to make in the class. Since he'd been teaching the same course for years, the initial (huge) investment in writing this all down paid off, eventually. I looked at him with a mix of shock and awe. "Not me," I thought.

Few professors these days practice the Socratic method in its purest form, whereby every question is met with another question, until finally, at the last branch of a large tree, the student gets to fall off and hit his head. Most of us settle for a much modified form.

Mr. Brown, the professor begins, state the facts of such and such a case. Then the professor eats Mr. Brown for lunch for omitting a critical fact, or including one that makes no difference. Why does that matter? she asks. Or what about X? she asks, focusing in on the one fact Mr. Brown has left out. Or she switches one little fact and asks him if it would matter. Or she asks him what difference a fact makes . . . and after she's made mincemeat of him for a while for including irrelevant facts or excluding relevant ones (what makes facts relevant or irrelevant, of course, being the legal issues), she moves on to those issues.

And what did the Court hold, Ms. Cohen? the professor asks, and then she eats Ms. Cohen for lunch if she misstates the holding, or doesn't realize that it's a plurality rather than a majority, or some such. Did they affirm or reverse? What's the rationale? Why? But what if . . . ? And what if, in the next case . . .

And then she takes the student down the "slippery slope." The slippery slope is the long road of hypothetical applications, of next cases, and next cases and next cases, until you get to the point where the new rule doesn't work anymore. And what do you do then, Mr. Smith? What happens to your rule now? If an hour is enough time to cool off from seeing your wife with another woman in the Mustang, what about half an hour? What about fifteen minutes? What about seven minutes? Five minutes? Where do you draw the line, Mr. Smith?

When courts say, "We need not decide in this case all of the future applications, blah blah blah . . ." it means they're avoiding the slippery slope. When they say, "Were we to hold otherwise, there would be no way to limit the application of this rule," it means they're using the slippery slope as an excuse. Old tricks.

> "Therefore" means not therefore.
>
> "We are obliged to follow precedent" means this makes no sense but we're doing it anyway.

WHAT SHOULD YOU REMEMBER WHEN YOU'RE CALLED ON?

The professor can always win. She knows more than you. Plus, there's no right answer. There's always a slippery slope in sight somewhere, or a ridiculous application of a rigid rule.

Whether you're partner or pawn depends mostly on you. Whether it makes you angry, or makes you want to prove that you're smarter than the professor or anybody else, or it makes you tense, or it makes you sick, or it brings out the best in you is up to you. Most professors want you to do well. They want to move the ball forward. If you're prepared, listen, and work with them, they'll help you; what's infuriating, frankly, is a student who won't listen, insists they're right and you're wrong, wastes everyone's time, etc.

In the moment when the professor questions a student in front of other students, she does have power. I think most of us try to respect that power and use it kindly, but that's for you to judge. Humiliating twenty-three-year-olds isn't really much of a thrill. Honest. We just want to teach. Treat us with respect, show that you've prepared and are trying, and we'll return the favor.

Give the professor an answer she can work with. Help move the ball forward. That's your job when you get called on in class.

What's most interesting about the next two stories is that they are about the same professor.

After my third week or so, an attorney from Mental Health Legal Services (or something like that) gave me the "only" good advice I've ever gotten regarding law school. He told me to not worry about it at all. If I didn't want to do the reading, don't. If I didn't want to go to class, skip it. If a professor calls on you in class and you don't know, look him in the eye and say, "I don't know. I have no idea," and don't worry about it. I tried this in [the former dean's] torts class, looked him in the eye and said I had no idea, and he sat there and stared at me for a solid fifteen seconds with the whole class in complete silence, and I just said, "Look, I said I didn't know, I don't know what you want me to do about it . . ." It was nerve-racking, but it made me much more relaxed about law school when I realized it didn't really fucking matter.

—MATT S., 3L;
USC

Rack this up among your typical first-year stories. I was unprepared for the reading one day in my torts class. But first, a little bit of background is needed: the professor was the former dean of the law school; he was heavily Socratic and consistently wore a bow tie to class. In his syllabus, he recommended doing each reading assignment three times. A truly engaging and masterful lecturer and teacher; I had the utmost respect for this professor. When I heard him call my last name one day, I thought I was prepared for the day's readings. However, I hadn't been prepared for the end of the previous day's assignment. My heart sank as I could only mumble that I was not prepared. When he said he could not hear me, I was forced to repeat myself. Needless to say, I wanted to disappear from my seat, or at least hide behind my laptop. Yes, I was embarrassed, but the more nagging feeling was that I felt I was letting the professor down—that my being unprepared suggested I did not value his teaching efforts. This was far from the truth, and I think that was why this particular incident stands out for me. Though it was my "worst memory," it reminds me how much I have begun to appreciate the education I am receiving in law school.

—MARK B., 2L;

USC

Ask anyone what he got called on about in his first year. He'll remember. I can tell you what I got asked about in property ("If you were lucky enough to find a rich husband, Miss Estrich, what state should you marry him in?" I picked California. Right answer was Texas.)

Chuck Weinstock can remember, too:

By the time I got to Harvard Law School, the Kingsfields were pretty much gone. Professors continued to use the Socratic method, but it was a kinder, gentler version. And if a student didn't want to play along, he or she was free to pass.

Still, there were a few holdovers, and my civil-procedure teacher, Arthur Miller, was one of them. He began his first lecture by saying that there were two words in the English language that he just didn't recognize: "I pass." He said that being a lawyer was all about intense preparation. He expected us to read and reread the assigned cases—to worry them to death—and then to be ready to spend a full hour talk-

ing about them. He ended his lecture with this: "I never met a lawyer worth his salt who was unprepared."

This put me in a state. Somewhere along the way, I had lost my nerve to speak in public. It was an odd terror; I had been the state debating champion in high school. But whatever the etiology, the fear persisted, and I genuinely dreaded this Arthur Miller class. Day after day, he would call on one student and rake him or her over the coals. It wasn't pretty.

It was the custom for each professor to invite a handful of 1Ls to lunch—a largely fruitless attempt to put them more at ease—and about a month into the school year, Miller invited me, among a few other students. To my surprise, he and I really hit it off. Near the end of the meal, I confided to him that I did not relish the prospect of speaking in front of a hundred and fifty of my classmates. He was surprised and said, "That's funny. You strike me as someone who might really like speaking in front of a hundred and fifty of your classmates." A shrewd assessment. There's always a little grandiosity in a fear like this.

Anyway, I went home that afternoon and began studying, because I was pretty sure Miller would call on me the next morning. Chessman that he was, though, he didn't. He called on me the day after.

I had read the assigned case, and if I had maintained some semblance of my senses, I could have muddled through the interrogation. But my head was swirling, and I said to him, "I think I'm going to pass." He reminded me that there was no passing in his class, but I said, "Still, I think I'm going to." He was visibly angry, and asked, "Why?" I said, "I'm psychologically unprepared," and he said, "I don't know what that means, Mr. Weinstock, but I expect to see you in my office within twenty-four hours." Then he called on someone else.

I was so depressed that I went back to my house and put on a recording of Paul Scofield reading Hamlet. It didn't help.

At the end of the day, I went over to Miller's office. He was standing at the far end of the room, talking to some lawyer in New York. His back was to the door, and he saw me in the window reflection. Without turning around, he signaled for me to sit down. He stayed on the phone for another ten minutes, never turning to acknowledge me, and I began to get really scared. Finally, he hung up, turned around, and to my great astonishment, gave me this big warm avuncular Jewish grin. In the kindest voice, he said, "What happened?" I said, "I told you. I'm no good in front of a hundred and fifty people." He said, "Look, I could give you a pass for the year, but really that's not what you need. I'll make a deal with you. You tell me when you're ready to talk, and then I'll call on you."

Well, I never told him I was ready to talk. But near the end of the year, I began to feel rotten about abusing his offer, so I went over to his office. I told him that, while I was by no means ready to talk, enough was enough, and he should just call on me. Tomorrow. He shook his head and explained that the case we were doing tomorrow was dull. "Let's do it Thursday. Parklane Hosiery." I said, "Fine. Parklane Hosiery." So I scurried home and got ready for Thursday.

Thursday came around and he didn't call on me. I assumed that this was yet another HLS mind game, and that afternoon I called and left an angry message on his answering machine. A pretty impertinent thing to do. Around eleven-thirty that night, just as I was getting ready to go to bed, Miller called me at home. "Chuck, this is Arthur Miller and I want to apologize. I had a family emergency this morning, and I just plain forgot about our deal. As far as I'm concerned, you've honored your half of the bargain, and you're off the hook." I went to bed relieved—but also a little sad that I hadn't just done the damn thing.

A few days later, Miller happened to pose a question to the class, and no one knew the answer. I did, and I figured, "What the hell." So I raised my hand to answer the question, and Miller and I had a nice long exchange. It was enough to get me over the hump.

That was twenty-three years ago. Chuck is a friend, a father, and an extremely successful movie producer in Los Angeles.

Most of the time, of course, you're not getting called on. You're just sitting there, listening to some other poor soul being eaten for lunch. You can be asleep or awake, paying attention or not. For that matter, you can not be there. Most law schools don't care. You're a grown-up now. You're on your own. Your grade doesn't depend on it a bit.

There are legendary stories of people who never showed up to class, walked in for the exam, asked if they were in the right room, rubbed their eyes, and proceeded to get an A-plus. People like . . . Susan Estrich.

Why does everyone like you always tell people to go to class? my editor wants to know. *What about all those people who never went to class and got straight A's?* First of all, that's not true first year. Those people don't exist first year. They don't start existing until second and third year. I know because I was one of those people. I never ever went to class. Ever. For most of two whole years.

This is what I was doing when I never went to class: law. This is what I was doing when you were goofing off: law. This is what I was doing when you were at the movies: law. The reason most of the people who never go to class never go to class is because they are working at law, usually at *Law Review*, in which case they are learning the essentials of fast writing, thinking, and analysis, albeit on their own. I've never worked harder. If you want to spend every waking hour doing law instead of just going to class and reading, enjoy yourself. Almost no one does very well without going to class unless that's what they do.

GO TO CLASS.

The point is to get as much as you can out of what you put in. You're not tricking us if we don't care.

SIT IN THE FRONT, IF YOU HAVE A CHOICE.

I know, back-benching is the cool thing to do. It's cool because that's where you sit if you think of class as a place to meet cool people, flirt, make friends, read the case for the first time, eat lunch, and play turkey bingo (What I did when I *did* go to class—with a group that included future well-known writer Mickey Kaus, as well as future law professors, Steve Ellman [Columbia] and Mark Kelman [Stanford], thus the name Ellman, Kelman and Kaus, as well as future editor Mike Kinsley.) How did we get away with it? Multiple choice:

A. Professional writer
B. *Law Review* zombie
C. All of the above

The assumption always is that if you sit in the back you are less likely to be called on by the professor.

First of all, this is not true. I always aim at the back of the room. Remember, we were all students once. Some of us were even back-benchers. In fact, you are more likely to fall asleep and get nothing out of class if you sit in the back and daydream. In the long run, this is not an efficient use of time. Since you're there, you might as well learn something.

ASSUME, EVERY TIME A QUESTION IS ASKED, THAT YOU'RE THE PERSON WHO HAS TO ANSWER IT.

Answer it in your head. See if you can really do it. See if you can do it as well as the person who is doing it. Otherwise, you may fool yourself into thinking that you know more than you do, only to discover later on that you know less than you think. And by that time, it may be too late to catch up.

WHAT SHOULD YOU DO IF YOU ARE UNPREPARED FOR CLASS?

The problem with calling on someone who is unprepared is that at best it's a waste of time, and at worst the professor could lose control of the class. If a teacher's been at it for a while, she doesn't worry about losing control.

But for new teachers, it can be a huge problem. Ultimately, as the student, you have no interest in being in a room that the professor doesn't control, and no real interest in contributing to his or her losing it. Quite the contrary, they'll probably succeed someday (and you might, too), and they could be in a position to help you along the way.

There is a very simple answer to what to do if you are *unprepared for class:* **Phone the professor's office in advance, or leave a note,** say you're coming but you're not prepared, apologize in advance, and say you don't want to waste his time and the class's by passing, and not answering fully.

WHAT IF YOU'RE HAVING
REAL PROBLEMS?

Go see the professor. We don't bite. But it's still worth it to cut a deal, not be called on, and come to class.

I do this with students all the time. It is much better to go to class unprepared, and let the professor know, than to skip altogether. You'll learn something being there. If the only reason you're thinking of not going is because you're unprepared, send an e-mail, leave a message, write a note, but go to class.

Law school is hard, particularly first year. It may not always seem that way, but classes help you understand the material, train your mind and your mouth.

{ 16 }

MASTERING THE FINE ART
OF EXAMSMANSHIP

Law school does not necessarily reward effort or hard work. It does not measure all kinds of skills that determine success in the real world. I cannot emphasize this enough. What law school mostly measures is a skill called examsmanship, or if you prefer, exams-person-ship. It is very much connected to being smart, and to success on the bar exam, but not necessarily connected to being a successful lawyer.

All other things being equal, writers do the best on essay exams.

The person who got the best grades in my class was a fellow named Stuart Taylor. You may see him on TV now and again or read his articles in newspapers or legal journals. That's because he is now, and was, before he went to law school, a very fine journalist. He writes incredibly quickly. In full sentences. In paragraphs. With opening sentences. Nouns and verbs. He could do this in the days before word processors, no less. My class boasts a number of federal appellate-court judges, congressional committee chairmen, senior partners in law firms, and many millionaires. Stu is neither the richest nor the most successful, as he'd be the first to tell you. But no one could write faster than he, which is why he got the best grades. As for me, I also did very well. Do you see what I do all day? Write.

The first step in any course is to pull together the material. Every first-year course is a mixture of doctrine, theory, and policy. How much of each depends less on the subject than on who's teaching it. In a space of fourteen weeks, meeting two or three times a week, you can cover only a limited number of doctrines. Each doctrinal issue will inevitably trigger a number of subissues. For instance, in criminal law, once you recognize you have a self-defense problem, you know you're looking at what the threat was, and was it imminent, and was there a cooling-off period; you know you have to look at whose perspective governs in evaluating the threat, and what the standard of reasonableness is, and which characteristics of the defendant will/won't be taken into account, and don't forget who started it, and whether there's any duty of retreat, or any special duties. Then you want to ask yourself, what values are we really trying to promote here? Is it respect for human life? Is that why we say, don't shoot unless you're in imminent peril? But remember you don't have to be right. And you don't have to retreat in your own home in general, even if you could do so safely. What value does that serve? Are all lives really of equal value?

The first set of questions in a first-year class on any topic will focus on establishing the doctrinal rules, and the tensions at the margins of those rules. That's what all the outlines are about.

What commercial outlines tend to do wrong is oversimplify: They look for a way to tie a tidy bow, to fit everything together, even if what makes law interesting is the tensions, and not always the fitting of them together.

Depending on how into "theory" your professor is, and most are—or why would they be law professors instead of making much more money being lawyers?—the last thing in the entire world they want is someone answering a question or approaching their course by tying together in a neat little box what doesn't fit together at all. You hear, or worse, read an exam answer like that and it makes you feel like, where has this student been all year? That's why people who rely on outlines get mediocre grades (not to mention the people who write them).

Say you have a class on self-defense. You'll read two cases. In one, the defendant will get off; in the other, he'll be convicted. There'll be all kinds of differences between the two, including the nature of the threat, the cooling-off period, the possibility of retreat, as well as the sympathy we feel. You leave class, shaking your head. What do you do?

You can wait until the next class, if your professor is one to sum things up at the beginning of the next class. You can go back over your notes, the case, and the hornbook your professor recommended, and you'll probably see it's all sitting right there, the basic requirements for the use of deadly force: an imminent threat of death or serious bodily harm to you or another; the difference between self-defense and provocation, the question of reasonableness. You make a list of each of the requirements, and what the issues are. This is what it means to begin the outlining process. You forget about the names of the cases, and the facts and the holding, and get with the doctrines, and the issues that are raised; the point of doing your own outline is to establish command of the material so that all you have to do is see self-defense and you can rattle off the subissues and you understand the issues they raise, so now we can start talking about reasonableness as the subtext that runs through the substantive criminal law, and the extent to which considerations of gender or efficiency or political dominance or whatever your professor is or isn't selling get in there.

Is it easy once you get the hang of it? Maybe not easy, but it's certainly a whole lot easier than it is in the beginning when you have to read everything two or three times and write it down sometimes just to follow it through. But everyone does get a fair amount of it, eventually. Just not all of it. As fast.

You have to outline. You have to physically do it yourself. By outline, I don't mean it has to literally be Roman numeral, followed by A, B, C, and 1, 2, 3 . . . but you have to organize the material. It's the process of working it out and writing it down, the doing of it, rather than the having of it, that makes it work. Therapy doesn't work if you read it. Neither does learning. And certainly not outlining. Or borrowing someone else's. I used to give my outlines away happily. Never worked for anyone else. You have to do it. That's the problem with study groups.

You outline by rereading the case against your class notes, against the best authority you can find, and putting it all together for yourself in an outline or shorthand form. Then you outline, or shorthand, or checklist, the outline. Then you make your checklist. So you have the course in one page, and in forty pages. You can look at a hypothetical against a checklist of the key concepts in the class. In back of each of them is a list of subquestions. In back of each of them is a policy context. You can spot the issues, do the back and forth, slice the bologna, analyze the doctrine, take it up to the level of policy and theory. You can forget about case names at this point (except in con law); you know you're dealing with rules and principles, doctrines of general application, values that underlie those doctrines, etc.

The answer doesn't matter. It's all how you get there. You're learning to be a lawyer, not a judge. It's not where you come out, in most courses, but how you get there. So even if a question asks for an answer, it usually doesn't matter: what you're going to be judged by is how many issues you see along the way, how you make the arguments, and the holes you see in them.

(The exception, of course: some professors now give multiple-choice questions in the first year.)

I read the following comment and I thought, "I have to include this because basically, he's right."

I wish I knew that the advice most "experts" on writing law school exams emphasize, setting aside a percentage of time to outline an answer before you begin writing it, was bunk. Here is why: if you have your outline memorized and then read it six times, as you read an exam question, all you have to do is jot down the issues that you are going to touch on (parole evidence, statute of frauds, third-party beneficiary, incapacity, surety, anticipatory repudiation, etc.). Then put them in the order you want to address them (usually the order in which they appear) and begin writing. After you write the issue statement, because you have the rule and all its elements memorized, writing it is the easiest part of the exam. The rule statement becomes your outline; it is the road map to your answer. Now just argue both sides of the rule using the facts of the question while mixing in a little common sense. Outlining an exam answer is nothing more than writing it twice; you should already have everything outlined in your head, this will save you time and give you time to grapple with issues no one else saw or had time to address. Write absolutely everything about each issue that is tested. No matter what the issue, write the rule, write what courts typically do, write about the policy issues you addressed in class, write everything you can think of, write everything, but never write "I think that . . ." unless specifically asked (who cares what you think, all anyone cares about is what the law is and what the judge will think). Out of the twenty-five or so exams I've taken, writing everything I possibly can has never not worked for me. Not conventional I know, but this works. I only wish someone had been honest enough to tell me all of this before I started law school so I wouldn't have had to waste a semester or two figuring it out on my own. I also wish someone had told me that generally speaking (especially when you are newer to the game), the better you feel you performed on an exam, the lower your grade will be and vice versa. Why is this true? If you felt you aced it, it's only because you missed several issues and failed to see the real tension between the parties involved. All you saw was the softball the professor threw you so that everyone would at least be able to write about something. There is no such thing as an easy exam. If you felt you barely had time to scratch the surface or didn't have time to touch on everything, it's because you saw all the tension and probably more than everyone else. Rest easy—you got an A.

—JAMES VEITH,
Fourth-Year Evening Division,
Widener University School of Law

Handwriting matters;
clarity matters; writing matters.

Type if you possibly can. How fast you can type and how well you write has a great deal to do with how well you do. You are not likely to be able to change these things. They will not necessarily affect how successful you are as a lawyer unless you go into appellate practice or litigation, but they will affect your grades. So there it is. If you have messy handwriting, and you insist on handwriting your exams, I promise you that you will never do as well as Stu. He typed. I had very neat handwriting. I have graded tens of thousands of exams in the last twenty-four years. When I complained about it, my first year of teaching, one of my colleagues told me it was the only honest "work" we did, and he was of course right, and I've never complained again. Reading the same answer 140 times, as I used to do when I taught big first-year sections, is work. There is absolutely nothing fun about it. There is nothing intellectually satisfying about it. There is a reason it's called work.

These days, I teach mostly to a roomful of laptops. If you can't type, learn. Especially if your handwriting is messy. If I have to struggle, it better be good. If I've worked twice as long to figure out what you've said, it better be twice as good.

My colleague Charlie Whitebread has written a fine little book about taking first-year exams that many law students receive for free as a sort of early promotion for the BAR/BRI Bar Review courses, for which Charlie is the star lecturer. It's an excellent basic text. It does not guarantee you an A.

Remember: It's not criminal law, it's criminal law with Professor Estrich . . .

As Charlie points out, the most important piece of advice is ultimately what he (and I) can't tell you: what your particular professor wants. That is what is wrong with every advice book that claims otherwise. I'm teaching you to think. This year, they asked me to "use" criminal law. Most of you won't be criminal lawyers. I happen to believe that it's my job to teach you enough criminal law that you feel some responsibility to the system; actually, I take that piece seriously because you probably won't be practicing it, and you may be leaders. But there I go again. The way I teach, the theories, tensions, policies— some would be the same if I were teaching contracts.

Part of learning to be a lawyer is understanding that what I want, as opposed to what the brand-new teacher next door wants, may be something different; you're expected to know that, just as, later in life, when you're dealing with different lawyers and judges, you'll be expected to size them up.

Most professors give essentially the same exam every year. That doesn't mean they ask the same questions, but the same kinds of questions, looking for the same kinds of answers. So once you've done your outline, outlined your outline, finished your checklist—in other words, once you've established command of the material—the best advice is to get copies of the professor's old exams (and ideally, the top answers) and go over them. Analyze them. Understand what they're looking for. Are they classic-issue spotters? Are they mixed-issue spotters—asking you both to spot the issues, analyze them, and also add in the policy and theory, or are policy and theory a separate question? Try answering the question. See if the professor is willing to review practice answers (many are, if you ask). If not, this is a good time for a study group, even if you've never been in one. Go over them together.

The most important thing to do after you read an exam is to take a deep breath, pause, and quickly outline your answer. I don't mean a real outline. The "outline" you do before you start writing is no more than a list—a checklist, so you know how much you have to cover.

- Organize by person, or by transaction; the important thing is to have a system and stick with it.
- Assign yourself a given amount of time per, and stick with it. Once you've decided on how much time you have per, be religious.

Fifty issues in fifty minutes means a minute per. The whole IRAC in a sentence or two. If you start writing before you make your list, I promise you that you will run out of time without adequately covering everything. Your first paragraph will fail to convey a sense that you know where you are going. You will get to the last question without enough time to answer it.

- The worse thing you can do is write "sorry time" at the end of the exam. Did I not notice that you ran out of time?
- If something important on your checklist is not on your exam, you're probably not seeing it.
- If something important on the exam seems to have nothing to do with anything, you're probably missing the point. As

a matter of fact, if there is any word, or factlet, on the exam that doesn't have some significance, you're missing something.

• If there is any issue from the course missing from the exam, you're probably missing something.

• If there is any subissue missing, you're probably missing something.

No Erie problem. No felony murder. Nothing on strict liability. Look again. Make a list.

Now here there is a difference of opinion. Charlie's book says to take twenty minutes to do an outline. I do not think you can take twenty minutes to do an outline and get a really good grade. *If you know your stuff, take seven minutes, and make a list;* maybe Charlie and I don't really disagree, except about how long it takes, and how much time you have left to write.

Know how much you have to cover before you start writing.

Decide how much time you have per issue. Scary. A one-hour question. Two dead bodies. Three guys. You're looking at five minutes a guy a killing. Not a lot of time. And you've got to deal with conspiracies and all that. How do you know how to approach it, without spending that extra thirteen minutes Charlie thinks you need?

Practice in advance. Most professors give virtually the same exams every year. Many will put sample or ideal answers on reserve from past years. Don't regurgitate. Imitate.

There are more than a few professors (my students tell me) who give precisely the same exam repeatedly—a multiple-choice one to boot, in one notorious case. On essays, however, no one pretends otherwise. Most essay exams are exactly alike with the only difference being the particular questions (law school humor, get it?). So all you have to do is practice on a professor's past exams and figure out what they want and give it to them. Some professors are even happy to go over it with you.

Take practice exams in a group.

Only one person is reading the exam. That doesn't mean you have to play to the professor's politics; not at all. You don't have to take a "liberal" approach because the professor is a liberal; most of us bend over backward not to play favorites in this regard. Quite the contrary: I remember, still, the law school exam I wrote for the most left professor as Justice Renchburg, my own combination of Burger and Rehnquist, to the right of both. Got an "A."

But we do want to know you've been to class, listened to what we've said, benefited from class discussion; you can take advantage of the shorthands that have emerged over the semester as a way of communicating problems, explaining tensions in the law, and the like.

Never write anything that sounds like it came from a canned package unless you know you have a professor who wants that sort of "bar stuff" in an answer. Be very very careful about this. If I smell *Emmanuel's* on an answer, I run for the hills, and I remember Steve's first civil-procedure outline, when Miller found the mistake in it and put it in the next year's exam, to catch everyone who was using it . . . Does that suggest an extreme version of my attitude? It's one thing if you read it, but don't expect me to. I hate reading exams, truth be told, I'm reading essentially the same thing over and over a hundred and forty times, and if instead of pulling things together to show the tensions or problems that I've tried to build into the question, you give me some canned black-letter junk from *Gilbert's.* It's a bathroom break, at least.

Use fewer words to show you're smarter. Analyze the argument and the defenses. Don't describe. From my perspective, all I can do in assigning a grade is, in effect, say to my friends in practice, or to whoever is judging you based on your grades, this is my recommendation based on reading one piece of a student's timed work. This was an A piece of work, versus a B piece of work or a C piece of work. There is a difference, without question; but it only applies to the piece of work I'm reading. I'm judging a piece of work, not a person.

What Are Professors Looking For?

Of course, what all of us want to know, first and foremost is:

1. That you understand the material.
2. That you can manipulate the material.
3. That you can write powerfully, make a powerful argument.

4. That you can integrate facts, law, and a little theory in a sentence, or at least in a paragraph.

5. That you can manage time.

6. That you show signs of having gone to class, listened, and learned some of what was unique to the professor's course, teaching, and approach.

7. That you can do all this in clear, concise English.

I have what I call "The First-Paragraph Rule." After two decades of grading exams, I have come up with various games that I play with myself basically to get through. My favorite in recent years is the first-paragraph game. I guess, after reading only the first paragraph of an exam, what the grade will be. I'm right, as it turns out, well over 90 percent of the time. Now I know what you're thinking: of course I'm right because I can make myself right. Wrong. I have all kinds of checks to keep myself honest. Sometimes I have little scoring systems, check marks for points that I total at the end, so I don't even know. Other times I just read the first paragraph, mark it down, and go back and read the exam later. It's not because I make myself right, but because the first paragraph almost always gives away most of what I just put on that list: whether a student is in command of the material, knows where she's going, has a plan for an answer, which is really no more than a list, knows how to do a paragraph that isn't 90 percent a waste of words, full of "I thinks" and facts that will have to be repeated . . . one paragraph can make me feel like I'm in good hands, or can safely recommend this piece of work to a friend.

MULTIPLE-CHOICE MADNESS

I'll make my bias plain. I hate multiple-choice tests. Most of them are stupid. Some people find it easy to write them and grading them is unbelievably easy. You need to pass them to pass the Bar, which is why some professors say they give them. Others argue that the fine lines we are asked to draw between exams in order to make the bell curve are impossible to do fairly—which is probably true, too—so they resort to an imprecise measure capable of being graded precisely. You're stuck taking them.

In studying for a multiple-choice test, you're obviously looking for rules, doctrines, things that can be right and wrong . . . to the extent such things exist in the law, but as I said, don't get me started. Remember the LSATs. Sorry.

Read the question very carefully. Look for wrong answers. Eliminate then guess. Same old. Look for the red herrings. Most professors aren't that good at writing these tests. Wrong things stick out. It's much harder to find the right answer than it is to identify the wrong ones. So if you're in trouble, eliminate.

On True-False tests, the conventional wisdom is always that your first instinct is usually right. So in guessing, when it's fifty-fifty (rare in law school land), go with your first instinct, unless the professor is known to be a complete jerk.

WHAT IF YOU'RE DISAPPOINTED WITH YOUR GRADE?

Learn from your mistakes, don't make a fool of yourself a second time.

- Everyone leaves something out.
- You can't win a fight about a grade.

Whatever you get, never ever complain that you got the wrong grade.

We all put way too much in our exams so when you come to see us and say, I got everything, we can look back and say, but where is X and Y and Z? We put things in that no one gets, that really are useful in making fine distinctions, not just dealing with students who can be obnoxious. So you will **always** have left something out.

What's more, to protect everybody, most schools do have rules that simply don't allow us to change grades even if we wanted to, so there is no point to being obnoxious, which may not be how you see yourself, but is almost certain to be how the professor will see you, which really is the last thing you need . . .

{ 17 }

HOW TO MAKE FACULTY MEMBERS LIKE YOU

Faculty members can seem very scary, especially to first-year students, who tend to obsess about their professors. I remember a student telling me, years later, that with another student one day he had discussed the fact that I had started wearing some pearls and concluded there must be someone special in my life. I was dumbfounded. The pearls were phonies I'd gotten at Loehman's.

There are some professors who play with this knowledge in all kinds of ways, who find pleasure in it, get off on it, swagger around classrooms, require a sort of adoration that makes doing anything more than understanding what you, as a student, need to know too much to ask for. It feels like they have all power over your life, like they know something you don't, like they can change your life with the stroke of an A.

Actually, it doesn't work that way. Blind grading means we read one exam and assign it a number. What professors can do, down the road, is mentor students, particularly if you don't get the top grades, help you find your place in the school, the profession, help you figure it out, get the interview, explain away the summer you didn't have a job.

Most law professors, even the most well meaning, have very large and very fragile egos. Consider: they had to do very, very well in law school to become law professors. But they are currently making less than second-year associates in middling law firms in large cities. The most junior partner in a good law firm in L.A. makes more money than I do working four jobs. How does this make me feel when a student walks in acting like he's smarter than I am and treating me like dirt? Not great. Even I want to eat him for lunch. And as I say, I'm nice, and fairly secure . . . You have to believe that what you're doing has some meaning to justify doing it. But if students tell you that you're awful, or act like their education is, it's hard to be nice.

What makes things worse is that most young, new professors aren't very good at what they do. This is the dirty little secret. It takes a while to get good at the job. Also, a lot of people don't want to teach first-year students. After a while (in my case, seventeen years is what it took), all that excess emotional energy gets exhausting. So schools are always drafting new blood in: most places, during your first year, you get a balance of young and old, good and not so good, experienced and not so experienced.

These days, if someone doesn't like my class, it's okay. But in my early days, it was not so okay. I can still remember, in my first year of teaching first-year students, going out and buying new clothes: a red dress, a red skirt, a red shirt . . . and on the third day of class, having a class full of students dressed in red. At least I'd been warned. Some women students tipped me off that a "clothes action" was planned. I'll always be grateful I was dressed in navy blue. I had a hypothetical ready, about a rapist in a red sweater . . . and whether that would be enough to stop someone on his way to a law-firm interview. Believe me, they laughed. I didn't. Did I hold it against them? Did it make me like those students less? Do professors hold grudges against students who are rude, insult them, try to prove that they're smarter than the professor? Absolutely. Even twenty years later.

IN DEALING WITH FACULTY, BE RESPECTFUL, TO A FAULT.

- When you go see a professor, say it is because you were confused, not because the professor was confusing.
- You must have made the mistake, not the professor.
- Go because you want to understand what you did wrong, not to complain about a grade.
- Go for help, not to bitch.
- Do not go to tell a professor, especially a new/young professor, that everyone hates her class, or that you don't hate it but everyone else does.
- Do not go to the dean to complain that the professor is late, confusing, difficult to understand.
- Do not go sit in on another professor's class in the same subject because you got stuck with the new teacher.
- Go to say you like class, want to do even better, just had one or two questions, was hoping to work for him this summer because you like it so much . . .

Be nice. Be polite. Be courteous. Say thank you. Be understanding. You will get absolutely nothing from being any other way.

THE EASIEST WAY TO GET A FACULTY MEMBER ON YOUR SIDE IS TO BE A RESEARCH ASSISTANT OR A TEACHING ASSISTANT.

My teaching assistants, who work with me on my undergraduate class, actually get tuition remission.

Everybody gets my help in whatever they want. To be honest, given what I do for my teaching assistants, I'm surprised more people don't apply. But they don't. Go figure. So be smart. Get a job that will pay big returns. Working at a law firm that will never ever hire you pays no returns . . .

The easiest way to get a job from a professor, of course, is to get the highest grade in the class. But the chances are that that person also got the highest grade in another class or two—and will be going to work for the best law firm in town, which suddenly found a space for a first-year student. So here's your opportunity.

Law professors tend to hire students who are not the best students in their classes to work for them in the summer because the best students go work for law firms. They hire someone competent who comes looking for a job. **Go looking.** Ask around. Some schools require you to advertise so all students have an equal chance. So you put up flyers. Even so, if someone has shown the initiative to come seek you out and tell you they want to work for you and why, it's still a big plus. It's different from always hiring the kid from Skull & Bones.

Mentors are hiding in other places in law schools. Many of them hide in clinical programs, in the adjunct faculty, in externships, in the form of administrators or legal-methods instructors, even in the form of 3Ls. Talk to successful people, and most of them have a mentor. Finding a mentor would certainly be on my list of the top three tasks you might set for yourself in your three years of law school.

{ 18 }

"HITTING THE WALL" IS PART OF THE LAW SCHOOL EXPERIENCE

It happens to almost everyone, although at different times. It could be about eight or ten weeks into your first semester when you decide that everyone knows everything better than you do, and low-level panic turns into full-fledged hysteria. You are never going to understand the material, never going to be ready for exams, never going to pass, never going to be a lawyer. The fact that there are a million lawyers in this country, many of them demonstrably dumber than you, is utterly irrelevant. You are ready to call home.

Or maybe you make it all the way through the first semester, assume you've done fine, take exams, all is well, and then you get your grades, and for the first time since first grade, the first time in your entire life, you are very clearly, absolutely, *not* in the top half of your class, and having made your peace with not attending your first choice law school, having decided that you'll do very well, and work at a top firm anyway, and show them, you now see clearly that your dreams are going up in smoke, your career is over, and you're ready to pull those sheets

up or head for the beach or call home, or start waiting tables or
open the tequila.

*I wish I'd known that so much of law school grading is arbitrary, and
working hard and knowing the material cold doesn't necessarily mean
you'll do well. That is a hard thing to swallow, especially since we all
did so well in college. I wish I had known (or believed those who tried
to tell me) that briefing every single case in every single class wasn't
worth the time commitment. I wish I had known I wouldn't have been
laughed out of class if I passed when a professor called on me.*

—H.D.M., 2L;
*University of Connecticut
School of Law*

Or maybe you make it all the way to the spring of your first
year, having gotten through first-semester grades by conclud-
ing that you did okay, and can do better next term, and now it's
April, and you've got four exams ahead, and there is no way
you're going to catch up, much less master everything you've
got to learn, and the turkeys in your section are already doing
their outlines, and you're still behind in the reading, and the
temperature outside is reaching ninety degrees and there's no
air-conditioning where you live, and your computer is crash-
ing every five minutes, and your parents just decided to get divorced after twenty-five years, and your father is dating someone
your age, and you don't have a job or a place to live for the
summer, and all you really want to do is sleep for an entire
weekend, and the way you've figured it, if you don't sleep at all
for the next three weeks, you just might have time to finish
doing all the reading, and you look around at all the second-
and third-year students, and you can't believe they made it
through this.

For some people, for all the talk, it comes later, when they can't find a job, get behind in everything, and no one even sympathizes anymore because you're supposed to be beyond this sort of thing after all; wasn't that just first year?

Or maybe you get hit from left field with something from the "real world" and you can't begin to figure out how to incorporate it into your law school world, and you're done in no matter what you do, because what kind of person cares about law school when her father is dying, and what will happen to you if you don't pay any attention . . . ?

To prospective law students—if you don't have the heart, go home. If you're here for the money, you'll quickly realize that it's not worth the nightmare of being a 1L. For those of you who have the heart, accept the fact that your first year will make you question every single thing you ever thought true about yourself. You will cry. You will contemplate quitting, in a very serious way. You will question your worth and ability as a lawyer. Your professors will push you to an intellectual level that you just don't think you're capable of. But always remember that it's supposed to be hard. If it was easy, everyone would do it—and would you really want to be a part of it then? You will be faced with two options: you can quit and remain the person you were when you entered law school, or you can stand and fight to attain the intellectual level you are capable of.

—T.C., 1L;

USC

When it happens, there are certain things to remember and do, and certain things not to do:

1. Look at all the second- and third-year students. They made it. They are not all smarter than you. Look at all the lawyers of the world. They are not smarter than you either.

Next year, you will be one of them. Next year, the wall will be in your past. Know that.

2. Take a night off. I don't care how much work you have. When you are facing a wall, it's impossible to read, study, or learn. You need to be at least far enough away from it that a book can fit in between you and it. You need to take a step back. Whatever you're doing can be done in a day less if you're in better shape.

3. Remember that what worked for you in the past will still work. If you've always crammed, you'll cram. You'll be writing motions at the last minute twenty years from now. That's life. That's you. The fact that the plan-ahead types plan ahead doesn't mean you will, or that you have to. Learn what you can. Come up with Plan B. Okay, so maybe you're not going to have time to brief every case. How about just reading every case?

4. Do not make any decisions when all you can see is a wall. How could you possibly be seeing clearly?

5. Go talk to someone. A counselor at the law school (every school has them for just this reason). A professor (we were all there once). Someone in the dean's office. It will not hurt your career.

6. Remember that there's more than one way to skin a cat. If you're desperate to work for a top-ten firm, then having top grades helps. I won't deny that. But it's not the only way. You can also find a professor or a judge to get you in the door, get in the door by going to a prosecutor's office first, by bringing business in, by winning moot court. You also might hate it . . .

7. Exactly why did you go to law school? Was it just to make money? Make partner? Is that what you wrote that great essay about? Can you remember? Is your property grade really the most important thing in the world?

8. Everybody graduates. There's a bar you can pass. You can

be a lawyer if you want to. If you don't, you don't have to be. There really is no gun to your head. Get help if you need it. Get through if you can. Get two nights' sleep and it will all seem easier. Time cures almost everything.

Every school has a soft touch like me.

I wish I'd known that it's okay to relax—your grades increase with your relaxation level. I wish I'd known that you have to take and pass a bar exam in each state in which you want to practice. I wish I'd known that "kissing up" works for some people; it would've been worth a try. I wish I'd known that it would fly by; I would have tried to enjoy parts of it more. I wish I'd known that there were other people who felt like crying every day the second semester. I wish I'd known that employers really don't care if you don't get a job that first summer; I would've gone on an exotic vacation. Most of all, I wish I'd realized that life is just too short to stress over that horrible torts essay exam for two months!

—D.E.M.,
Recent Graduate;
University of Florida,
Levin College of Law

A woman in my section attempted suicide. My friend Suzanne noticed she wasn't in class. She went looking for her, banged on the door, got security to let her in, called the paramedic.

That's the other thing. Keep an eye on one another.

First year ultimately ends.

None of my friends can understand me because I find it "objectively practicable" to insert extra syllables into words that do not appear to need them. (I also like to "unpack" Law & Order episodes for my friends, which they find very useful.) And if everything goes according to plan, in a couple of years, more than half the world will think that I only put my hands in my own pockets on really cold days. But . . . after your last final first year, someone will inevitably say: "Now, you are a 2L." You will look around a little bit and think, "Who is this guy talking to?" Then you will realize, it's you. It was harder than Rollerblading backward up Mount Everest while yodeling (or maybe just as hard), but this guy is talking to you. That is when you'll think: Finishing First Year? Totally priceless. If you don't live in SoCal, you might leave out the "totally."

—Priya Chatwani, 2L;
USC

My personal statement to Yale was about why a Yale undergraduate with a degree in political science summa cum laude wanted to go to law school not graduate school. I quoted Montesquieu, God help me, about how often political theory convinces everyone and affects no one. I wanted affect.

Brown v. Board of Education was what I had in mind, and it was a rude shock to discover, even at Yale, how little of legal education and legal practice is like that. I found the first semester in law school extremely intimidating and irrelevant to why I had come. The low moment was having to draft a contract for a hypothetical swimming-pool-furniture manufacturer and negotiate it with another class member who was smart enough not to reinvent the wheel and presented me with an alternative (a thinly adapted version of her Macy's charge-account agreement).

I spent my first-year law school exam throwing up in the ladies' room and I almost left law school for a fellowship in political theory in

England. What kept me in school was work in a poverty-law office, which turned into a large empirical survey about access to nonlawyer services.

I began to see law as a way to write about justice, and I have been doing that more or less happily ever since. But the other low moment was summer work in a fancy firm, where I had to spend two weeks reading condemnation cases in an effort to convince some administrative-law judge that our client, the owner of a chicken ranch (Julius Goldman's Egg City) hit by a chicken disease deserved a better compensation rate for his dead chickens. The fact that I can still dredge up many details (I heard a lot of chicken jokes during those weeks) speaks volumes about memories still not entirely repressed.

—DEBORAH RHODE
Professor of Law
Stanford Law School
Author, Report of the ABA Commission
of the Status of Women
Former Supreme Court law clerk,
and great friend and feminist

You do what you have to do. There is an expression in Yiddish: *Ba'shert*. What is meant to be. I asked many, many people if they "hit the wall" in law school.

One response sticks in my mind. The woman said that she wasn't really familiar with the phrase, but she'd had a very tough time second year. Her husband and classmate—they'd recently married—got very sick; he had to have life-threatening surgery. She declined *Law Review* and ultimately transferred. He recovered; they have been married more than forty years. She was the second woman appointed to the United States Supreme Court, Ruth Bader Ginsburg.

{ 19 }

HOW TO GET THE MOST FROM YOUR LEGAL EDUCATION

WHAT IF YOU MAKE *LAW REVIEW*? WHAT IF YOU DON'T? WHAT NEXT?

This is the easiest question in the book: If you are invited on, or have a chance to write on, the *Law Review*, YES. (I actually read one advice book that said to think twice; guess who must still be smarting.)

Advice? That grades are the most important thing and that I should try to be on Law Review. *The advice was helpful, because my grades have been paramount in the job search, as was being on* Law Review.

—ANONYMOUS,
Fourth Year in Joint JD/
MBA Program; USC

In selecting my courses, I only took subjects I thought I would be interested in. I was unconcerned with the official recommendations, and so I never took corporations, commercial transactions, accounting, securities law, family law, estate planning . . . I did take the basic tax course, but it was an experimental, policy-oriented course rather than a serious course. I took advanced antitrust law, but never took basic antitrust. My attitude, frankly, was that I would learn what I needed to learn for the bar exam by working very hard in the bar review course. And I assumed that when I got into the real world, if there was a field of law for which I needed some basic background, I would take a week and read a couple of books, not unlike cramming for an exam. So my attitude toward course selection (and attendance, for that matter) was that of an unapologetic dilettante. I saved my rigorous attentions for my wholehearted efforts on the Law Review. *Now, as a faculty member, I believe students should do as I say, not as I did.*

—Christopher F. Edley, *Dean;*
University of California
Berkeley School of Law

The advantages of any law journal, but especially "the" *Law Review* at your school, are substantial. It opens doors. *If you want to clerk, work at a big, high-paying firm, or teach, it's the first step.* Especially if you are not at a "top" school, doing *Law Review* adds a lot. It's prestigious. It's a niche. You learn a lot. You become an ace footnoter. You work incredibly hard. It may seem like busywork at first, but believe me, knowing how to write, cite, and edit, getting to work with faculty, getting your work published, become a first-rate cite checker and blue booker—these are not skills to be sneezed at. So absolutely yes.

> Try out for the *Law Review*. People will just as-
> sume you are smarter than you are if they see *Law
> Review* on your résumé, and the truth is you will
> be guaranteed to learn good skills that way.

And if you don't make it, is your life over? No. Larry Tribe
didn't make *Law Review.* Neither did Kathleen Sullivan, currently the dean of Stanford Law School. Barney Frank, the
congressman from Massachusetts, who was in my class, turned
it down. He was in the state legislature at the time. Too busy.
Bill Clinton didn't do *Law Review.* He did fine, too.

**Half of the people in law school are destined to finish
in the bottom half of the class.** Almost none of them did so
as undergraduates. It is not easy to make peace with that. In
many cases, you will find that there is very little you can do
about it. When you get out, you will feel smart again.

WHAT IF YOU DON'T MAKE *LAW REVIEW*?

Find other places to excel, explore, and connect. Use law
school for all it is worth.

- Look for an organization to run or start.
- Find an externship in the real world that you can get
  credit for.
- Find a mentor inside or outside the law school.

- Find a niche, a group of like-minded people, a corner of the building where you can leave your things and hold on to yourself.
- Connect with lawyers/alumni in the community who share your interests/politics/passion.
- Use the law school in every way you can.

EDUCATE YOURSELF IN WHAT YOU NEED TO KNOW.

In the first year, everybody complains that we treat them like babies. In the second and third years, they complain that we don't take care of them at all. Welcome to the world. You're in charge of your own legal literacy, and I don't just mean Business Organization and Gifts, Wills, and Trusts.

Writing is important no matter what you do.

Lawyers should know how to research and find answers to everything.

I also think, in the future, they should understand politics and economics and the worlds of business, speak foreign languages, know how the world works—that "international" is in this year, as the most recent special rankings issues of *U.S. News & World Report* documents. Law schools are tripping over one another to establish international programs and partnerships as are law firms themselves.

Why? Student interest. Firm interest. Foreign governments that will pay full fare. Prestige. Doing the right thing. All of the above. But that may just be because of my interests. Which brings me again to my most important point: **What you need to learn in law school is what you want to do with your life.** What your first job should be. What you're doing there, if you didn't already know. What you care about more than money and prestige. Who you want to be.

Believe it or not, after the first year, it moves fast. No one tells you anything. You do what you want, basically. You can discover you're two credits short two days before graduation. In that respect, it is not like high school. Students get lulled.

One of the easiest things to let happen in law school is a form of semiparalysis. You stop making your own decisions. You take whatever courses everyone else is taking. You know the list. You do moot court because everyone else is (even though you meet no one, and don't care about it). You spend the summer after your second year working at a firm you would never work at permanently because you didn't get an offer at one of your first-choice firms and didn't have enough initiative to find something better. You're in a groove, okay—but it might as well be a rut.

The power of your law degree will come, ultimately, in what you bring to it. Find out what else you can study in the university and still get credit. Become an educated person if you can. Yes, there's still time. Take interesting courses. Get involved in the local community. Make sure to cultivate faculty members who can help you in areas you care about by taking repeat/seminar/research courses; this is in almost every case much more important than the subject matter. Experiment with passions. Look for ways to get out of the library and try to interact with people whose lives you can try on. Try to become more of yourself. If you blow the job-hunting season second summer, find something to do nights that makes money (tend bar) and days do something you might care about, at least. If you don't have a clue, find a solo you admire, and go carry his or her briefcase. See what being a real lawyer is like. Go do something useful. Work two jobs. Make the day one be your new mentor. The night one pays the bills.

A lot of law students are very ambivalent about being where they are. They settle in, and crawl along, unhappily. They aren't sure they're in the right place, and unfortunately, that becomes an excuse to look backward instead of forward. It's "Did I do the right thing?" instead of "Where am I going?"

Chances are, if you've made it past first year, you're going to end up with a law degree. Your second-year tuition is probably already paid for by the time you start asking these questions. Your third year, if you're clever about it, you can get through, with some easy courses and independent work. And then what? Life. Who is kidding whom? **The goal of law school is not to get through, but to get as much out of it as you can.** The measure is *you:* what it does for you, in helping you achieve your goals, by your lights, according to your yardstick, not anybody else's. What's that? It depends—on what you're there for.

Say you decide, going into third year, that you don't want to be a lawyer. So what? You have one year left. You will have a law degree. You can either spend the rest of your career with the credibility of a law school graduate or explaining why you dropped out. Someday, if you are a multimillionaire, it will not matter. Until then, it may. Someday, if you change your mind, and need to make a living, it may matter more than you can imagine. Finish the year. Use it to figure out smartly, thoughtfully, and passionately what comes next. Write the screenplay, don't complain that you have one in you. Sit down and do it. Learn Chinese if you think that is where you're headed. Use the place. You want to be a journalist, take over the school paper for your last year, be splashy, and you'll have your next job.

Money is what makes law a limiting profession. We all know that. The minute you have to earn a certain six-figure salary, whatever it is, you place your hands in cuffs, which makes it exceedingly difficult to escape; still not impossible but now really really hard; and then you suffer. The reason most people go down that road is not, interestingly enough, because they choose to, want to, decide to, think it is best; it is for want of anything else to do.

If you begin your third year of law school no further along in understanding who you are or what you care about than when you started, you're likely to end up working for the biggest and best corporate firm that hires you, a duplication of the application process. Only this time, all the jobs aren't fundamentally the same, in the way all law schools are; you don't learn the same thing wherever you go, and there isn't anybody who will hold your hand then.

You'll soon be on your own. Why not take advantage of all the help you have until then.

IS THERE SUCH A THING AS FUN/LIFE IN LAW SCHOOL?

Culture: I would guess it is most schools, but it could be just mine. It is high school—almost nothing like my undergrad experience. We have classes with the same seventy people, five days a week. The school makes our schedule and planned it so that we are on campus from about nine to four. The whole school shuts down for an hour at midday so that everyone can have lunch, and we have a cafeteria with bad food and rude service. We have lockers and mailboxes. The boxes are often stuffed with info from different clubs—there is the environmental club, the women power club, the sports-and-entertainment club, the justice club, the Hispanic club, the Black club, the Asian club, the animal-lover club, the cops-suck club, etc. However, the only club that gets any sup-port whatsoever is the public-interest club. More power to them, but if you are not in law school to save the world, the administration could give a crap about your interests. We also have the student bar associa-tion, which is just ASB all over again and people campaign by giving out lollipops and putting up funny posters. We have a dance in the spring that was eerily similar to prom, and the professors fall into the stereotypes as well—there is the crusty prof who complains of his ex-wife, the crazy one who runs around the room and will do odd things to get your attention. The scary prof who challenges you to push your-self and the crazy lady who answers every question with a question while running her hands through her hair, and it ends up in odd con-figurations that are more interesting than the class.

Friends: people who go to law school are not cool. If you think you are cool and are looking for cool friends, don't come here. I never thought I was cool, and in real life I am not really, but in law school I feel like an edgy, trendy superstar. Cool in law school is Chandler on Friends *or Will on* Will & Grace *—not a dork, but you know he's never been really cool before. In law school, he's a freaking rock star—Ozzy Os-bourne, James Dean, and Frank Sinatra rolled into one. People who are the shy quiet people don't speak and leave quickly. It's an odd mix.*

WHAT ABOUT DATING IN THE OUTSIDE WORLD? LAW STUDENTS?

Personally, I didn't have time to date. A lot of people come to law school with serious relationships (actually it seemed the majority did to me). As for dating law students, if you do it, be careful! Think of it like high school—you are in the same classes with usually no more than two hundred people, everyone knows everyone else, and so in our school, there were a few people who dated within the class and everyone knew all of the details.

For example, there was a guy, let's call him Aidan, and Aidan started out with a girlfriend not at our school. He then cheated on her by making out regularly with Jenna, a "friend" of his from school. After a Thursday-night bar run, he slept with Kristy, from one of the other sections. Then he and Jenna slept together, and three months later he was sleeping with Laura. I am not friends with any of these people and rarely went out, but I know all of these details because it is like high school all over again.

• • •

I met a boy right before beginning school. So I decided not to commit until I had a chance to check out the law school boys. Let's just say I'm now in a very committed relationship.

• • •

I ended up dating a guy from law school the first semester of my first year. It was a good time and I really liked him a lot, but it was really hard see-ing him every day for the rest of the year. We were still friends after the breakup, but it was still superweird. It also didn't help matters that every-one knew about the relationship and everyone is in your business about it.

• • •

I dated a lot of people outside of the law school during the year, but that sucked. No one really quite understood that I needed to study most of the time and I couldn't party as much as I would have liked.

• • •

Ha. First semester, dated one boy in the law school, in my section. Bad idea. Definitely should've heeded that advice about not dating anyone in your section. Wasn't very experienced with relationships to begin with, so was learning a lot about boy-girl relations/romance, etc., along with my contracts. Dated about a month and a half. Dramatic breakup. Division of mutual friends. He started dating someone else in the section. Drama.

• • •

Second semester. You would've thought I would've learned the first time to not date anyone in the section. But alas, I started dating another boy in the section. This time, the breakup was even worse. However, this guy indeed might have had some emotional issues. Started dating at the beginning of the semester; he broke up with me just before finals. Evidently, three months later, this gentlemen is still not over the relationship.

If I were to do it over again, I would probably not date anyone in the law school my first year. Unfortunately, I didn't know any other person in L.A. besides my classmates, so it was inevitable that I would end up dating one of them. Ahhh well. It's over. Stuff was learned, and I survived.

• • •

My girlfriend is from the outside world and we did find it difficult to spend time together. I'm sure trying to date someone new outside law school would be next to impossible.

• • •

WHAT'S A TYPICAL DAY LIKE FOR YOU?

A typical day for me starts with a quick overview of the cases I need to know for class that day. It's very cursory, nothing too intense. Then, classes, break, more classes, and then the trip home for the afternoon. I generally like to read for a little while then head to the gym for some downtime, after which I'll generally come home and finish all my reading. If I have a lot of extra time, I'll generally take at least half an hour to outline a bit and overview the material we went over in class. When all that is done, I just like to hang out with either my friends or my girlfriend (or both at the same time). Sometimes it gets pretty intense, time-wise, but I figure it's law school and I knew what I was getting into when I decided to take the LSAT.

—ADAM WOLFSON,
University of Michigan
School of Law

DIVERSITY?

I was shocked at how parochial some of my fellow students were/are. Some have never encountered African-Americans like me . . . If the student is a minority, I would remind them that this isn't college . . . and that hopefully they picked a law school that is supportive and has a strong minority community. Why do I say this? Because racism creeps out in graduate school. People who might have been quiet in college now speak their mind and the administration can be as hard-line as they choose all under the auspices of proving how "hard" law school is. Furthermore, I would suggest that they think about whether they care about what people think—because law school is just as petty and psycho as high school.

—M.J.W., 3L;
Tulane Law School

SEX? MAYBE IF YOU'RE FIFTY-TWO . . .

I was a returning student—fifty-two years old when I went to law school—so the advice I received may be different than that received by younger students. Advice: Keep balance in your life. Remember your family but don't expect to see them very often. Take time for sex. Don't let the first year kill you.

—Victoria L. Grace, 4L;
University of Baltimore

KILL YOU? IT REALLY DOESN'T HAVE TO.

Law school is a great, great experience . . . not only do you learn the law, but you learn how to handle stressful situations. You can either go in being obsessed or dedicated. If you are the former, it will eat you up and take control and your performance will suffer. You need to be dedi-

cated: take control of law school like you would a job. See law school for what it is: serious, difficult, time-consuming, but not everything. I would always say, "I don't have an hour for the gym," or "I don't have time to grab a drink." In retrospect, when I did sacrifice some reading and did those things, I was much better off. Because there is so much work, if you have that attitude, you will never "finish." So taking time is crucial for two reasons: 1) to blow off steam, get endorphins flowing, etc., and 2) it helps you learn one of the most important lessons of law school: to do something well in a finite amount of time. For example, you need to set, say, three hours to do torts, no more, then move on . . .

—PAUL ROSEN, 2L;

USC Law School

I would tell them that 1) don't give up after your first semester . . . it all gets better from there; 2) you will meet some of your best friends in law school whom you will truly remember (and see again); 3) take yourself seriously, but be able to sit back on a Friday afternoon and have a couple beers and relax.

—JENNIFER A. SULLIVAN, '03,

Florida State University

College of Law

{ 20 }

FACING THE JOB MARKET

"I'm going to be a partner at Cravath," Phil Gelston announced about thirty years ago, when I didn't have the slightest idea what Cravath was. Now he is a partner at Cravath. Some people know. And succeed. Most don't. And don't. Thus begins the downhill slide.

From the moment you realize that you're going to survive, you begin thinking/obsessing about what you're going to do when you get out. There's no time to enjoy getting into law school . . . First you're terrified. Then you're disappointed. Then you've been rejected all over again, for jobs you didn't even dream you wanted, at places you didn't know existed. Why would anyone set themselves up for this? The answer is that it is almost impossible to resist.

Very few people write in their law school applications that they are applying to law school because they want to be partners in one of the largest and most successful civil-law firms in America. This is not what people say in their interviews, e-mails, or conversations with faculty. But it takes over like a fever from the beginning of the second semester of the first year.

It used to be that no one even expected to get a law job their first year. I did, off my first-semester grades, which made hitting the wall all the more terrifying; but it was a rarity. Today, the truth is that a lot of students don't find good law jobs the first summer, but the fact that more and more firms do recruit first year makes those students who don't get jobs feel worse about it. Freedom becomes failure. First-semester grades seem larger than life, even if very few people will end up at the firm they worked at first summer. I have fond memories of Stroock & Stroock & Lavan, where my grades meant $375 a week, an unheard-of sum for me, which also meant not having to bartend during the week the next year.

WHAT DOES EVERYONE ELSE KNOW?

One day, you've never heard of them. The next day, you'd kill to work for them. Who are they?

TOP 20 LAW FIRMS IN THE NATION BASED ON PRESTIGE		
1	Wachtel, Lipton, Rosen & Katz	New York, NY
2	Cravath, Swaine & Moore	New York, NY
3	Sullivan & Cromwell	New York, NY
4	Davis, Polk & Wardell	New York, NY
5	Skadden, Arps, Slate, Meagher & Flom LLP and Affiliates	New York, NY
6	Simpson, Thatcher & Bartlett LLP	New York, NY

(continued)

TOP 20 LAW FIRMS IN THE NATION BASED ON PRESTIGE		
7	Cleary, Gottlieb, Steen & Hamilton	New York, NY
8	Covington & Burling	Washington, DC
9	Latham & Watkins	Los Angeles, CA
10	Weil, Gotshal & Manges LLP	New York, NY
11	Kirkland & Ellis	Chicago, IL
12	Shearman & Sterling	New York, NY
13	Paul, Weiss, Rifkind, Wharton & Garrison	New York, NY
14	Williams & Connolly LLP	Washington, DC
15	Debevoise & Plimpton	New York, NY
16	Sidley Austin Brown & Wood LLP	Chicago, IL
17	Gibson, Dunn & Crutcher	Los Angeles, CA
18	Arnold & Porter	Washington, DC
19	Wilmer, Cutler & Pickering	Washington, DC
20	White & Case	New York, NY

Source: The Vault 2003 Associate Survey, <www.thevault.com>.

20 MOST SUCCESSFUL LAW FIRMS IN THE WORLD (2002–2003)			
	FIRM	LOCATION	GROSS REVENUE
1	Clifford Chance	International (UK)	$1,467,000,000
2	Skadden Arps Slate Meagher & Flom	New York	$1,310,000,000
3	Freshfields Brukhaus Deringer	International (UK)	$1,200,000,000
4	Linklaters	International (UK)	$1,080,000,000
5	Baker & McKenzie	International (US)	$1,060,000,000
6	Allen & Overy	International (UK)	$970,500,000
7	Jones Day	National (US)	$908,000,000
8	Latham & Watkins	National (US)	$906,000,000
9	Sidley Austin Brown & Wood	National (US)	$831,000,000
10	Mayer, Brown Rowe & Maw	National (US)	$705,000,000
11	Shearman & Sterling	New York	$700,000,000

20 MOST SUCCESSFUL LAW FIRMS
IN THE WORLD (2002–2003)

	FIRM	LOCATION	GROSS REVENUE
12	Weil, Gotshal & Manges	New York	$688,000,000
13	White & Case	International (US)	$675,000,000
14	McDermott, Will & Emery	National (US)	$628,000,000
15	Sullivan & Cromwell	New York	$624,000,000
16	Kirkland & Ellis	Chicago	$611,000,000
17	Akin Gump Strauss Hauer & Feld	National (US)	$575,000,000
18	Davis Polk & Wardwell	New York	$570,000,000
19	Gibson, Dunn & Crutcher	Los Angeles	$569,000,000
20	O'Melveny & Myers	Los Angeles	$565,000,000

Source: The Global 100, American Lawyer Media, November 2003, <www.law.com>.

20 LARGEST LAW FIRMS

	FIRM	NO. OF LAWYERS
1	Baker & McKenzie	3214
2	Jones Day	2136
3	Skadden Arps Slate Meagher and Flom	1827
4	White & Case	1681
5	Latham & Watkins	1624
6	Sidley Austin Brown & Wood	1559
7	Mayer, Brown, Rowe & Maw	1376
8	Morgan, Lewis & Bockius	1196
9	Holland & Knight	1164
10	Weil, Gotshal & Manges	1125
11	Shearman & Sterling	1089
12	Greenberg Traurig	1023
13	McDermott Will & Emery	1002
14	Akin Gump Strauss Hauer & Feld	977
15	O'Melveny & Meyers	974

(continued)

20 LARGEST LAW FIRMS *(continued)*

	FIRM	NO. OF LAWYERS
16	Morrison & Foerster	971
17	Kirkland & Ellis	958
18	Hogan & Hartson	957
19	Reed Smith	957
20	Piper Rudnick	946

Source: The NLJ 250, The National Law Journal, <www.nlj.com>.

TOP ELITE LAW FIRMS PER CITY

Atlanta
King & Spalding
Alston & Bird
Kilpatrick Stockton

Boston
Hale and Dorr
Ropes & Gray
Goodwin Procter

Chicago
Kirkland & Ellis
Sidley Austin Brown & Wood
Mayer, Brown, Rowe & Maw

Cleveland
Jones Day
Baker & Hostetler

Dallas
Akin, Gump, Strauss, Hauer & Feld
Haynes and Boone

District of Columbia
Covington & Burling
Williams & Connolly
Wilmer, Cutler & Pickering

Houston
Baker Botts
Fulbright & Jaworski
Vinson & Elkins

Los Angeles
Latham & Watkins
Gibson, Dunn & Crutcher
O'Melveny & Myers

Miami/Florida
Holland & Knight
Greenberg Traurig

Milwaukee
Foley & Lardner

Minneapolis
Dorsey & Whitney

New York
Cravath, Swaine & Moore
Wachtell, Lipton, Rosen & Katz
Sullivan & Cromwell

Philadelphia
Morgan, Lewis & Bockius
Dechert
Drinker Biddle & Reath

(continued)

TOP ELITE LAW FIRMS PER CITY	
Pittsburgh	**San Francisco/Bay Area**
Kirkpatrick & Lockhart	Morrison & Foerster
Portland	Wilson Sonsini Goodrich & Rosati
Miller Nash	Orrick, Herrington & Sutcliffe
Stoel Rives	**Seattle**
Richmond	Perkins Coie
Hunton & Williams	Davis Wright Tremaine
McGuire Woods	Foster Pepper & Shefelman
San Diego	**St. Louis**
Gray Cary Ware & Freidenrich	Bryan Cave

Brian Leiter, *The Most National Law School Based on Job Placement in Elite Law Firms,* Educational Quality Rankings of U.S. Law Schools: 2003–2004 (July 1, 2003) <http://www.utexas.edu/law/faculty/bleiter/rankings/03_most_national.html>.

LET'S TALK ABOUT DEBT

• In 2003, the average law student graduated with close to $90,000 in debt.

• Starting salary of first-year graduates in law firms with more than 150 lawyers: $95,000.

• Starting salary of first-year graduates in law firms with twenty-one to forty lawyers: $65,000.

• The national average salary for all first-year attorneys, including those in public interest, is around $50,000.

There you are. You're in debt. Who isn't? You've never had a job that paid you $1,000 or even $2,000 a week. If you're like most students, this is a ton of money. Who can resist? Before you know anything or are worth anything, someone may be willing to pay you $2,000 to be wined and dined and sit in box seats at sports events.

In 2002, equity partners billed an average of 1,729 hours, while associates billed an average of 1,869; in the largest firms, the equivalent numbers were 1,820 for partners and 1,969 for associates.

(National Association of Law Placement, see 87 MAR A.B.A.J. 42,45 2001; 149 *Chicago Daily Law Bulletin* 133, July 9, 2003 [reporting on survey by Altman, Weil Inc].)

You look at the chart below. You show it to your significant other. You're five years away from earning how much?

ASSOCIATE YEAR	FIRM SIZE—NUMBER OF ATTORNEYS						
	2–25	26–50	51–100	101–250	251–500	501+	ALL SIZES
First	$59,500	$71,000	$80,000	$85,000	$102,000	$113,000	$93,190
Second	$64,500	$75,000	$82,800	$87,000	$105,000	$120,000	$94,000
Third	$67,250	$81,000	$85,700	$92,838	$110,000	$128,417	$99,250
Fourth	$72,000	$85,000	$89,513	$95,500	$114,000	$135,000	$105,000
Fifth	$81,400	$89,000	$92,500	$100,450	$118,900	$144,500	$110,000
Sixth	$95,000	$99,000	$98,650	$104,000	$126,125	$147,688	$120,000
Seventh	$95,000	$99,750	$101,666	$110,000	$133,250	$157,500	$120,875
Eighth	$106,000	$100,000	$105,000	$110,000	$143,150	$165,000	$124,900
1st-yr summer ($/week)	$865	$1,100	$1,538	$1,500	$1,925	$2,250	$1,750

MEDIAN BASE SALARIES BY ASSOCIATE YEAR AND FIRM SIZE (2003)

(continued)

MEDIAN BASE SALARIES BY ASSOCIATE YEAR AND FIRM SIZE (2003)							
ASSOCIATE YEAR	FIRM SIZE—NUMBER OF ATTORNEYS						
	2–25	26–50	51–100	101–250	251–500	501+	ALL SIZES
2nd-yr summer ($/week)	$924	$1,250	$1,500	$1,500	$2,000	$2,275	$1,730
3rd-yr summer ($/week)	$943	$1,200	$1,300	$1,500	$2,050	$2,375	$1,920

NALP Foundation, *2003 Associate Salary Survey* (August 8, 2003) <http://www.nalp.org/nalpresearch/sumch03.htm>.

The advantages of working at a big firm for the summer, in addition to the money and the baseball, are that you get to peek at law-firm life, without making a commitment; you also get to impress other people with that entrée on your résumé ("I see we're both Covington alums," people still say to me . . .), and don't have to do near as much work as you would if you actually worked in a law firm for three months.

The advantages of working at a big firm long-term are interesting, challenging work, sometimes; partners you respect, often; a place in your city's power elite; a very, very comfortable income; good vacations and hobbies; stability, sometimes; and quite a ride. There are more, I'm sure, but it's not what I do, so I'm not the best one to ask.

But here's the truth: nothing I say here will change your mind, one way or the other. By the end of first semester, all but the most resolute begin to head down a certain path and most of those who can get these jobs, do. Those who can't end up feeling bad that they can't.

One of My Most Fun Days:

Unfortunately, even trial work can be pretty dull. There are few dramatic courtroom moments à la The Practice or Ally McBeale. Once in a while, however, you can get off a "zinger." When it is in a good cause, it feels even better. While I was still a Big Defense Firm Lawyer, I once had a defamation case in which I represented a state university and one of its fraternities. The latter had, as part of its fund-raising activities, printed up and sold a coed pinup calendar along the lines of Girls of Animal House. Some of the photographs were rather racy posed pictures, while others were just random photographs of girls walking around the college campus.

One of the girls in one of the "nonracy," unposed photographs sued the fraternity for defamation, under a theory that including her photograph with the "racy" shots implied that she was a Woman of Easy Virtue. Her lawyer was a local nitwit who seemed to have a bee in his bonnet about the fraternity, and the university on which it was located. His briefs were incoherent; even worse, he belonged to the Bombast School of Litigation.

Every summer The Firm would assign the more junior, young-turk partners four or five summer associates, whom we were supposed to evaluate and convince to come to work for The Firm after they graduated. Most of these summer associates could barely write in English, and simply created more work for the attorneys. On top of that, most were arrogant little swine from the more prestigious law schools, and seemed to think that they were doing us a favor by agreeing to be paid enormous first-year-lawyer salaries for being taken to lunch, dinner, and social events.

One of these kids, however, turned out to be a real keeper. Tim was attending UVA Law School, and could write well. He still was really interested in improving his skills, and was a joy to teach. He was smart as a whip, worked hard, and—impossible to believe—was a really good guy.

About halfway from the summer, the word went out that the only way Tim would not get a job offer was if he killed someone in the lobby of the building (assuming The Firm could not pin the blame on someone else or dispose of the body). Tim, however, wanted to be a "real trial lawyer." He was from the South, and he was not particularly impressed by the business litigation cases The Firm usually handled.

We really wanted to keep Tim, so the junior partners were told to get him involved in the few "fun" cases that we had in the office, in an effort to show how "exciting" it would be to be a lawyer with The Firm.

One of the "fun" cases was my Animal House case. I thought we could get the lawsuit thrown out before trial, and Tim drafted up the summary judgment motion we were going to use to get rid of the case. He did all the research, and thought of it as "his" case. He could not argue the motion before the court, but I took him to the hearing so he could have the excitement of being in court on something on which he worked.

The court had a lot of things on its calendar that day, and the courtroom was packed with attorneys. The judge wanted to hear from the coed's attorney first, and he went into a rambling argument that wandered over the legal issues. He then paused and, as a rousing closer and in ringing tones, told the judge: "It's like those famous lines, Your Honor: 'He who steals my purse steals trash! . . . But he that filches from me my good name . . .'" etc. With these deathless words, he sat down.

According to Tim, halfway through the quote I turned to Mr. Bombast with this "really weird" look on my face. When he finished, I gave the judge my already prepared, "canned" presentation: Mr. Bombast is 1) wrong on the law, 2) wrong on the facts, 3) is wearing a really bad suit, and (whoa!) 4) check that hairpiece!

With that, I was done. I started to sit down, and then thought,

"You'll never forgive yourself if you let THIS *opportunity go by." I straightened back up and said, in My Most Judicially Deferential Voice: "Oh, one last thing, Your Honor? I appreciated Mr. Bombast's quote, but I'm a little puzzled. As I am sure the Court is aware, those lines are from the play Othello, and are spoken by the character Iago. As I also am sure the Court is aware, Iago is, with the possible exception of Richard III, the greatest villain and hypocrite in Shakespeare."*

I then closed, Sincerity and Puzzlement Positively Oozing From Every Pore: "Perhaps the Court understood what Mr. Bombast meant by that, but I sure as hell don't."

I kept looking straight at the judge, but I could see Mr. Bombast out of the corner of my eye. He looked like he'd been poleaxed. "Got him," I thought.

In contrast, His Honor sat there, absolutely impassive. Several seconds ticked by, and I thought I was going to get a blast from the bench. Suddenly, however, the judge's lip began to twitch. He tried to control it, but ultimately lost it completely and started laughing out loud. Given this judicial approval, the attorneys in the audience burst into uncontrolled laughter. They were still laughing when the judge ruled in our favor and threw the case out.

It would have been fun to nail Mr. Bombast regardless. That Tim was there to witness it made it all the better. He took The Firm's offer, partially on the strength of my performance. Tim ultimately made partner, but then threw up all the money and prestige to go do capital appeals as a matter of principle.

As I said, he was a good guy.

—J. NEIL GIELEGHEM
Attorney, Los Angeles

ATTRITION RATE FOR ALL NEW
ASSOCIATES HIRED FROM 1991–1998

PERCENT OF NEW ASSOCIATES LEAVING WITHIN:	1 YEAR	2 YEARS	3 YEARS	4 YEARS	5 YEARS	6 YEARS	7 YEARS	8 YEARS
Overall (5,486 hires)	8.3%	23.0%	38.3%	50.5%	59.6%	66.2%	70.8%	73.3%
ACCORDING TO OFFICE SIZE:								
50 or fewer attorneys (416 hires)	7.7	24.1	40.2	47.7	53.8	60.6	60.2	65.9
51–100 attorneys (732 hires)	10.8	26.4	42.6	50.6	59	64.3	70.6	72.3
101–250 attorneys (1,675 hires)	9.3	24.3	37.2	47.3	57.6	63.6	67.4	71.4
251 or more attorneys (2,190 hires)	7.3	22.6	40.3	56.3	65.6	72.8	78.6	78.3
ACCORDING TO DIVERSITY:								
Men (3,135 hires)	7.6	21.7	36.4	49.1	57.5	63.9	69.1	71.7
Women (2,272 hires)	9.3	24.5	40.4	52	62.1	68.4	72.5	74.6
Minority men (309 hires)	12.9	36.2	55.7	66.2	70.1	78.5	82.4	82.1
Minority women (306 hires)	11.4	28.1	46.5	63.7	74.1	83.6	88.9	100
ACCORDING TO CLASS YEAR:								
1991 (637 hires)	7.2	18.4	33.1	48.8	59.7	67.2	70.3	73.3
1992 (567 hires)	7.4	18.9	35.1	49.6	61.6	67.4	71.4	
1993 (566 hires)	5.3	19.4	34.8	48.2	57.4	63.8		
1994 (559 hires)	9.1	22.5	39.5	52.2	59.9			
1995 (681 hires)	6.8	26.1	42.4	53.3				
1996 (728 hires)	10.3	28.4	43.1					
1997 (800 hires)	9.1	24.9						
1998 (948 hires)	9.8							

Note: Figures show attrition of new associates from their first law firm after law school.

See NALP Foundation, *Beyond the Bidding Wars: A Survey of Associate Attrition, Departure Destinations and Workplace Incentives* (September 2000), selected tables available at http://www.nalpfoundation.org/webmodules/articles/anmviewer.asp?a=65.

The days when getting the first offer was the hard part are over. Getting to be a partner is the hard part, and it's getting harder. In general, the bigger the firm, the faster and the more associates leave; in the largest firms, 80 percent leave within seven years. For firms of every size, departure rates have increased steadily in the last ten years, as have billable hours.

All firms are not created equal. I had a student last year, *Law Review*, top grades, the whole nine yards, who came very close to being unemployed when the once-great firm she had an offer from went belly-up. Could she have seen it coming? Let's put it this way. . . . she was one of the lucky ones, who had another job before the implosion. My friends saw it coming, I told her, and we went to work finding her a new job before the hundred other associates started looking . . . Be smart about this.

If you're going to go the firm route, be informed. Check out the surveys. Equality exists only at the bottom. Most of the firms in a big city pay almost the same amount to starting associates, but that doesn't mean—not by any stretch—that they're the same down the road. Know what you're signing up for. There's a chance you may be staying for a while, and it matters. And—this is critical—even if you're one of the 60 percent (firms of fifty or fewer) to 80 percent (firms of 250 or more) who is likely to be leaving within seven years, your experience while you're there (not to mention the question of whether the firm will last that long) depends on its financial stability, client base, how happy the partners are, and whether their staying partners are expected to keep working as hard as associates at many firms these days, to keep billing 2,300 plus hours, to keep bringing in clients, and not just servicing them.

TOP 20 LAW FIRMS IN THE NATION
BASED ON QUALITY OF LIFE

1	Winston & Strawn LLP	Chicago, IL
2	Morrison & Foerster LLP	San Francisco, CA
3	Wachtell, Lipton, Rosen & Katz	New York, NY
4	Ropes & Gray	Boston, MA
5	Davis Polk & Wardell	New York, NY
6	Jenkins & Gilchrist	Dallas, TX
7	Alston & Bird LLP	Atlanta, GA
8	Haynes and Boone LLP	Dallas, TX
9	Debevoise & Plimpton	New York, NY
10	Jenner & Block	Chicago, IL
11	Finnegan, Henderson, Farabow, Garrett & Dunner	Washington, DC
12	Fish & Richardson P.C.	Boston, MA
13	Hale and Dorr LLP	Boston, MA
14	Troutman Sanders LLP	Atlanta, GA
15	Gray Cary Ware & Freidenrich LLP	Palo Alto, CA
16	Orrick, Herrington & Sutcliffe	San Francisco, CA
17	Jones Day	Cleveland, OH
18	Arent, Fox, Kintner, Plotkin & Kahn	Washington, DC
19	Cleary, Gottlieb, Steen & Hamilton	New York, NY
20	Allen & Overy	London, UK

Source: The Vault 2003 Associate Survey, <www.thevault.com>.

CALIFORNIA'S TOP 10
(BY PROFITS PER PARTNER)

Gibson, Dunn & Crutcher	$1,105,000
Latham & Watkins	$1,055,000
O'Melveny & Myers	$945,000
Paul, Hastings, Janofsky & Walker	$875,000
Wilson Sonsini Goodrich & Rosati	$855,000
Orrick, Herrington & Sutcliffe	$765,000

(continued)

CALIFORNIA'S TOP 10 (BY PROFITS PER PARTNER)	
Cooley Godward	$715,000
Morrison & Foerster	$675,000
Pillsbury Winthrop	$665,000
Brobeck, Phleger & Harrison	$660,000

Source: *The American Lawyer,* July 2002, <http://www.law.com/special/professionals/amlaw/2002/ca_top_10.shtml>.

All practice areas are not created equal. See L. Abrams, *The Official Guide to Legal Specialties,* National Association for Law Placement, 2002 (a publication of the BARBRI group, by the way).

SALARIES ACCORDING TO PRACTICE AREA SPECIALTY (ALL SALARIES ARE AVERAGE TOTAL COMPENSATION)		
SPECIALTY	ASSOCIATE	PARTNER
Administrative	$135,081	$276,854
Banking	$120,250	$313,027
Bankruptcy	$108,023	$265,619
Bankruptcy Litigation	$138,924	$293,796
Commercial/Contract	$118,773	$301,166
Commerical/Contract Litigation	$112,563	$253,333
Education	$92,779	$248,524
Employee Benefits	$123,098	$266,969
Employment	$106,675	$261,009
Employment Litigation	$108,195	$222,749
Environmental	$112,471	$232,199

SALARIES ACCORDING TO PRACTICE AREA SPECIALTY (ALL SALARIES ARE AVERAGE TOTAL COMPENSATION)

SPECIALTY	ASSOCIATE	PARTNER
Environmental Litigation	$118,701	$257,579
Family and Domestic	$90,453	$257,470
Family and Domestic Litigation	$97,788	$185,311
General Business	$102,977	$238,764
Health care	$102,337	$256,597
Health-care Litigation	$92,423	$233,922
Insurance	$92,015	$236,200
Insured Defense Litigation	$84,871	$207,512
Intellectual Property	$167,319	$350,601
Intellectual-Property Litigation	$162,611	$337,659
Labor-Management	$113,462	$269,587
Labor-Management Litigation	$104,827	$248,175
Mergers and Acquisitions	$109,815	$340,294
Municipal Finance	$119,580	$310,756
Natural Resources	$125,818	$241,798
Natural-Resources Litigation	$102,573	$303,723
Personal-Injury Litigation	$99,400	$304,236
Products-Liability Litigation	$114,802	$300,439
Real Estate	$115,504	$276,010
Real-Estate Litigation	$118,763	$220,540
Taxation	$119,608	$276,911
Trusts/Estates/Probate	$93,609	$217,904
Trusts/Estates/Probate Litigation	$100,088	$232,450
Workers' Compensation	$86,525	$185,794
Utilities	$105,409	$229,059

Altman Weil 2002 Survey of Law Firm Economics, The National Jurist, January 2004, at twenty-nine.

In terms of dollars, plaintiffs' lawyers who work on contingency (taking a percentage of the recovery) are the only lawyers who make real money. They are the only ones who come to Bar Association meetings on their own planes. John Edwards was a plaintiff's lawyer. That's how he made enough money to run for president and learned to move a room.

Big firm work demands a certain kind of intensity; even when it looks easy . . .

When I was headed toward my first summer clerkship, a partner at a big Atlanta firm advised me to "take a message to Garcia." That's the title of an early-twentieth-century book about a guy who endures various trials to take a message to Garcia in the Cuban mountains. He advised me to do what was asked of me, and then to do a little bit more in some way. It is a good admonition, no matter what the project.

Did you ever have a job you hated?

Modern discovery, catfights and all. I escaped by becoming a full-time teacher for three years, then developing a practice, which is mostly appeals.

Would you go to law school again?

Yes. The more important decision point was what to do after our clerkships ended. I'm glad [we] came back to Jackson to practice law. I've been pretty successful—my victory rate in the Fifth Circuit hovers around 80 percent—but I wonder whether some sort of column writing might be a direction to head in now. I've written several for the local paper, and had a short piece in the ABA Journal on amicus briefs. I've also got a book on peacemaking in the works. My reading for it has taught me a lot, whether it ever gets published or not. But we have three children to get through college and I really enjoy the very unusual group of partners with whom I work, so I'll be on the docket for at least a decade more.

Extra: People who want to be litigators should understand that, to be in that business, you have got to be able to enjoy personal conflict *(emphasis added by SE, who really doesn't).*

Also, in the lawyer-eat-lawyer world of modern litigation, ethics may be the most important course a law student takes, especially now that the ALI has turned most ethics rules into tort rules.

One summer I worked at a newspaper in the Mississippi Delta. They let me cover the courts. I decided I would rather be doing the law rather than just reporting what someone else was doing. After another summer as a journalist, spent at the Washington Post, I went to law school. Later I found life in a law firm much more congenial than I had found life in the Post newsroom, where everyone was competing with one another for the front page. Law firms compete, but for the most part, it is with the adversary rather than within the firm.

—LUTHER MUNFORD
Former Supreme Court Law Clerk
Attorney, Partner, Jackson, MS

LARGEST PLAINTIFF VERDICTS OF 2002

RANK	AMOUNT	CASE TYPE	CASE NAME	PLAINTIFF'S ATTORNEY	DEFENSE ATTORNEY	STATUS
1	$28,000,000,000	Fraud, products liability	*Bullock v. Philip Morris Inc.*, Los Angeles Super. Ct.	Michael J. Piuze Law Offices of Michael J. Piuze Los Angeles	Peter K. Bleakley Arnold & Porter, Washington, D.C.	Pending appeal
2	$2,225,000,000	Personal injury	*Hayes v. Courtney*, Jackson Co., Mo. Cir. Ct.	Eischens & McCreight, Kansas City, Mo.; Davis, Bethune & Jones, Kansas City, Mo.	David R. Buchanan Brown & James, Kansas City, Mo.	Pending motions
3	$520,770,000	Antitrust	*Kinetic Concepts Inc. v. Hillenbrand Industries Inc.*, W.D. Texas	Akin Gump Strauss Hauer & Feld*	Ricardo G. Cedillo; Robin P. Hartman Davis, Cedillio & Mendoza, San Antonio, Texas; Haynes and Boone, Dallas	Settled
4	$505,000,000	Breach of licensing agreement, unfair competition	*IGEN International Inc. v. Roche Diagnostics* S.D. Md.	Wilmer, Cutler & Pickering Washington, D.C.*	Nancy J. Sennett and John R. Dawson Foley & Lardner	Pending appeal
5	$500,200,000	Breach of contract	*City of Hope National Medical Center v. Genentech Inc.*, Los Angeles Super. Ct.	Irell & Manella, Los Angeles*	Robert A. Van Nest and Susan J. Harriman Keker & Van Nest, San Francisco	On appeal

*Hot shot firms doing plaintiffs' cases.

(continued)

LARGEST PLAINTIFF VERDICTS OF 2002

RANK	AMOUNT	CASE TYPE	CASE NAME	PLAINTIFF'S ATTORNEY	DEFENSE ATTORNEY	STATUS
6	$276,000,000	Breach of contract, fraudulent inducement	*Steele Software Systems Corp. v. First Union National Bank,* Baltimore City Cir. Ct., Md.	Snyder, Slutkin, Lodowski & Kopec, Baltimore	James E. Gray Venable, Baltimore	Pending appeal
7	$270,050,000	Personal injury	*Johnson v. Equitable Resources Inc.,* Knott Co., Ky., Cir. Ct.	Blackburn Gary C. Johnson, Pikeville, Ky.	Robert M. Connolly and Ian T. Ramsey Stites & Harbison, Louisville, Ky.	Settled
8	$261,700,000	Breach of fiduciary duty	*Burns v. Prudential Marion Co.,* Ohio Ct.	Starr Austen Tribbett Myers & Miller, Logansport, Ind; Maddox Hargett & Caruso, Fishers, Ind.	Samuel A. Keesal Jr. and Terry Ross Keesal, Young & Logan, Long Beach, Calif.	Pending motions
9	$225,000,000	Product liability	*Benavides v. Ford Motor Co.,* Duval Co., Texas Dist. Ct.	Wigington & Rumley, Corpus Christi, Texas	Jaine A. Saenz; Rosewell Page III	Pending motions
10	$185,090,000	Securities fraud	In Re Real Estate Associates Limited Partnership Litigation, C.D. Calif.	Chimicles & Tikellis, Haverford, Pa.; Goodkind Labaton Rudoff & Sucharow, New York	Robert J.A. Zito Fischbein Badillo Wagner Harding, New York	In motions

Top 100 Verdicts, 2002, The National Law Journal, February 2003, <http://www.law.com/special/professionals/nlj/2003/
national_law_journals_largest_verdicts_2002.shtml>.

WHAT IF YOU'RE DESPERATE FOR A FIRM JOB, AND DON'T HAVE THE CREDENTIALS TO GET IT?

If you're aching for that top firm job and you don't have all the aces—the right school, the right grades, the right recommendations, etc.—is there any way to get it?

Try for a part-time judicial clerkship during the school year, and see if you can get them to fall in love. Find a partner who went to the same undergraduate/law school as you, write to him/her directly, and explain why they should interview you anyway. Try to get a clerkship/internship/externship and get your judge to call for you. Find a professor who will call over to the firm for you. Pick the one firm you are dying to work for, and run a campaign aimed at them. Explain why hiring you will improve their softball team, why your grades don't reflect your potential.

Demonstrate what clients you can bring to the firm! Remember that these days, being able to bring business to the firm is more important than being able to write briefs. If you can make the case that you would be an ace rainmaker, they'll find somebody else to do the footnotes.

THE SECRET OF TWENTY-MINUTE INTERVIEWS:

Everyone is alike. After a while, you can't remember whom you've talked to. Your mouth hurts. You're tired. You're hungry. You start thinking about lunch. You wish someone would say something interesting, show some initiative, prove that the firm for them was more than an entry on the computer list. I practiced law for a year at a Los Angeles law firm (one that no longer exists). They sent me back to Harvard to recruit. I spent two days interviewing. It was mind-numbing.

Most students had done absolutely no preparation for the interview. They just showed up. It was a waste of their time, and mine. Like everything in life, if you want it, you need to go for it. Unless you have perfect grades, or are *Law Review* editor, or some such, you probably will find yourself with a résumé that looks very much like the résumés of the other twenty people that person has talked to that day. You have to sparkle, remember?

You have to use those twenty minutes to convince the person you're talking to that you really want to work at that firm, and that you have something to add. She knows what your grades are (they have to be on the résumé, regardless of what the rules are, or you won't get hired), she knows what your activities are, now tell her what you can do for the firm.

WHAT IF YOU DON'T FIND A LAW-FIRM SUMMER JOB?

Who said you wanted one? Pretend you didn't. Explore another opportunity instead. Work for a professor. Find a mentor. Do public service, etc. You think of it.

WHAT IF YOU DON'T GET AN OFFER AFTER WORKING FOR THE SUMMER?

Requires careful attention. Find lawyers within the firm who will help you, a version of the truth you and they can live with, a lesson you can take from it, a reason you didn't want it.

ARE THERE PEOPLE WHO FIND
HAPPINESS AT BIG FIRMS?

Absolutely. Look at the ruling class of any big city and you'll see top lawyers from top law firms. The guys (and that's what they usually are) who end up as the best in these big law firms are mostly very smart, sure of themselves, hardworking, smooth, tough, and self-confident. They make a lot of money, many of them are active in civic activities, generous to charities, good golfers, even.

If that's who you want to be, go for it.

REMEMBER THAT MOST BIG FIRMS NOW DO A
GOOD DEAL OF THEIR HIRING LATERALLY.

That means they hire between year two and retirement. Based on what you've done, who you bring, where you're going, not where you went and what you got.

This is one of my favorite stories in the book:

P.S. Grades don't matter—I mean you should try your best and obviously you have to pass, and some people will walk around tooting their own horns that they were in the top of the class. But who cares? Oh, some firms will care, but honestly—that's about it. After my first semester of law school, I got my grades and began packing my things to go home because I didn't receive the marks I thought I would get, or thought I deserved. Literally, I was talking to my mom on the phone telling her I was on my way home. Mom, being the wiser, talked me into staying. I wasn't even in the top 25 percent of my class, but guess what? I was elected editor in chief of one of the school's law journals, ran a student group, and became involved in the community—the key

I think being able to juggle extracurricular activities. I landed an awesome job with the government—they didn't care about my grades. Then I found a job with a midsize, prestigious civil-litigation firm and guess what? They never asked for my grades either. Now I am working for a big firm with great benefits and people I think I am really, really going to like, and you know what else? They never asked for my grades either. Grades do not have to control your life. Without stellar grades you can find a good job; and in my experience a good personality and hard work go a long way for serious employers.

—NICOLE A. BOLSON, '03;
University of Oregon

A SPECIAL NOTE TO WOMEN:

Where to begin? I wasn't supposed to be writing this in 2003. Things were supposed to be equal now. It should be possible for women as well as men to work in firms, be good parents, and good lawyers, without feeling like they are constantly forced to choose, up against the wall, lying to everybody, competing for the chairmanship of the Negligent Mothers' Club (a job I have held for years).

There are exceptions. Perhaps there will be more by the time you read this. But most large law firms have not done nearly enough to accommodate to the realities of the lives of most women who are mothers—and the result is that most of those women don't become partners, or don't stay; they become "of counsel," contract attorneys, or quit altogether; the ones who make partner don't have children, or never see them.

I have been teaching gender discrimination for more than fifteen years now, and follow these trends closely, and women are stuck in the counsel roles, dropping out before they come

TOP FIRMS BASED ON
FEMALE EQUITY PARTNERS

FIRM (RANK BY PROFITS PER PARTNER)	2003— FEMALE EQUITY PARTNERS/PERCENT OF TOTAL	1993— FEMALE EQUITY PARTNERS/PERCENT OF TOTAL	CHANGE IN PERCENT, 1993–2003
Davis Polk (4)	30/20.7%	9/9.7%	113.3%
Dewey Ballantine (17)	21/17.9%	9/8.1%	121.6%
Skadden, Arps (9)	54/14.6%	35/15.0%	-2.4%
Debevoise & Plimpton (14)	18/14.5%	6/6.6%	119.9%
Weil, Gotshal (13)	25/14.5%	18/12.8%	13.3%
Gibson, Dunn (14)	36/14.3%	27/11.3%	26.4%
Wachtell (1)	10/12.8%	6/11.1%	15.3%
Willkie Farr (12)	17/13.8%	10/9.2%	50.2%
Chadbourne & Parke (19)	12/13.6%	8/10.0%	36.4%
Paul, Weiss (6)	14/13.2%	6/6.4%	106.4%
Latham & Watkins (18)	50/12.4%	N/A*	N/A
Cahill Gordon (3)	7/12.3%	2/3.7%	231.9%
Simpson Thacher (5)	18/12.2%	8/7.8%	55.9%
Cleary, Gottlieb (11)	18/11.2%	8/6.7%	66.9%
Proskauer Rose (20)	17/10.8%	11/9.3%	16.4%
Cadwalader (14)	8/10.3%	5/6.3%	62.8%
Sullivan & Cromwell (7)	15/9.9%	6/5.9%	67.3%
Cravath (2)	7/8.9%	3/4.1%	116.1%
Milbank, Tweed (8)	7/6.9%	7/6.5%	6.6%
The following firm declined to provide separate numbers for equity and nonequity partners.			
Kirkland & Ellis (10)	65/18.4%	22/23.6%	-22%

* The firm did not provide separate numbers for equity and nonequity partners in 1993.

Measuring the Power, The American Lawyer, June 2003, <http://www.law.com/special/professionals/amlaw/2003/measuring_power.shtml>.

up for partner, not making gains at the top of this profession, partly because of the remnants of unconscious sexism, but most important, because a big firm is not an easy place to be any kind of a mother.

Does that mean you should give up? Absolutely not. Just know. Do not go gently into the night. Ask the tough questions about maternity leave and part-time partners. Ask to meet women partners who are also mothers. Take note if there aren't any, and you want to be one. Ask why not. What do you have to lose?

Laurie Levenson, Associate Dean and Professor of Law Loyola Law School

Did you ever have a job you hated?

I despised my summer law-firm job when I was in law school. Frankly, I hated everything about it . . . and they hated everything about me. I remember that the firm wanted me to go to lunch with the surviving "named" partner at the California Club. Then I learned I would have to walk in an alley entrance reserved for women. I declined the invitation and they weren't too thrilled. Suffice it to say, I decided to never work for a firm.

THE "YOU CAN'T GO WRONG
AT A BIG FIRM" THEORY ...

The "you can't go wrong theory" holds that the best training, and the best credential for any future job, is a big-firm job. U.S. attorney's offices hire from big firms. So do other firms, public-interest offices, Capitol Hill offices, public defenders, etc.

There are any number of limits to the theory: in fact, many people do go wrong. They are miserable. Or they are not miserable enough. They don't leave soon enough. Or they're more unhappy than they bargained for. Or they put the silver hand-cuffs on, and cannot take them off.

Ann Coulter,
Bestselling Author
and Columnist

Did you ever have jobs you hated?
    "Yes, and jobs I loved—both at law firms. Depending on which partner I was working for, a job at the very same law firm could be the best job I ever had or the worst job I ever had. The key to happiness is having a smart boss—or no boss at all. There is nothing more excruciatingly painful than having a nitwit looking over your shoulder and micromanaging your work. That is the definition of hell. Of course, having

an idiot superior who wrecks your work or requires pointless effort is obviously a danger with any job that involves a boss, but I think law firms tend to have more tyrannical morons than the average workplace. A lot of partners are miserable because they are working all the time. A law partner can never relax, he is always and forever tied to billable hours. All his friends at investment banks make a lot more money and rarely work weekends. So a lot of law partners are burning with resentment and frustration and often their decisions are driven by ego rather than by what is best for the client. Also, a partner's income is directly tied to how many hours his associates work. Completely useless make-work for associates means he can afford to join that fancy club—where he will rub shoulders with investment bankers and develop more resentments. Or perhaps there is something about the law that attracts a disproportionate share of bitter little people. Whatever the root cause, partner egos can lead to behavior that is absolutely incomprehensible to associates, who are still basically normal people trying to do a job. Oh and BTW, this sisterly camaraderie is a crock. I'm sure there are some great female law partners, but a lot of them are freaks and horrors. My mentors were always men.

THE SMALLER THE FIRM, THE MORE CAREFULLY YOU NEED TO RESEARCH IT.

Small firms come in every shape and size. Some are harder to get jobs in than the biggest and the best. Some are, despite all appearances, a heartbeat away from total financial default. What is striking to me is how oblivious students are to the differences, how focused they are on minute differences in starting salaries—only one indication of long-term stability, or anything else. I see students send out hundreds of résumés in the scattershot system in which they will end up working at the one who happens to respond to their casting call. Now imagine picking a hairdresser that way.

"But the others aren't interested in me," you're about to say. Well, what's to be interested in? How much of an effort have you made? All you've done is send a piece of paper, a cold résumé to an anonymous person—you're about as interested in them as they are in you. If you have no more interest than to send a standard form letter to "Recruiting Chair" or whatever it is . . . unless you're coming home from Harvard, you're going nowhere.

This is almost a complete waste of time, and what's more, guaranteed to produce you the worst possible job from the group, the one at the firm most likely to have hired someone who is not as smart as you, which will leave you most likely to feel bored.

Sure, you have to work. But you should be working with people whose professional ethic you share; whose integrity you respect; whose character is above repute. You're talking about associating yourself with a professional partnership that will define you as much as the law school you went to, eat up your time, and potentially your soul.

The smaller the firm, the better you need to know each of the lawyers in it. It doesn't mean you need to "like" them in the sense of: Would I choose to go to the movies with them? Or seek advice about my personal life? But would you hire them to represent you? Because if the answer to that question is no, you shouldn't be working there. Period. Stop. Don't work for people you don't respect. Don't work for lawyers you wouldn't want to represent you. Do something else. You demean yourself and you don't learn anything. More than a so-called second-tier law school, working for someone who has a terrible reputation is not a wise career move, and strategically speaking, it matters where you start. This is how you become an unhappy lawyer.

If you're going the small-firm route, devote enormous energy to research. Think about this as a huge investment of human capital (yourself) in a very high-risk company. Small firms can be great places to learn, or nightmares.

Whom do you ask? Everyone you can. Students will say to me: "Oh, they're a spin-off of so-and-so . . ." and I respond: "Did they spin off as partners, or associates? Good or bad terms? Are they getting referrals from their old firm?" They look at me blankly. It matters.

Every law school has a hidden resource that students never use. Adjunct professors are often extremely successful lawyers who decide that it might be fun to teach on the side. Students, most of whom are always afraid—with some reason—that adjuncts will be terrible teachers who will grade too hard, don't use them for what they are in fact best at, and what people in the real world in fact pay them dearly to do: give advice. Go see the adjuncts from practice. Don't ask them for a job. Ask them for an advice as you get yourself one. Let them guide you like they do the titans.

I wish I had known more about the job-hunt process and how what you did in law school related to it. One thing that was seriously lacking was individualized career counseling. Students were herded into corporate interview programs and no one really asked anybody what they wanted to do and devised individual plans for helping them achieve their goals. It was a shock to many students, including myself, how little help you would actually receive in the job search if you didn't want to work for one of the firms/agencies that came to on-campus recruiting.

—M.B.G., '01;
University of Michigan

Before entering law school, I was cautioned by my mentors that law school often drains creativity and passion. I ignored these warnings, sure that I could make my way in law school without changing my perspectives. By the end of three years of Harvard Law School, I found that it was true that I thought more logically and less passionately. I also found it difficult to be as creative as I had in the past. However, while passion and creativity are not often practiced in law school, I found it possible to keep these aspects of my personality alive through extracurricular pursuits. Further, upon graduation I was able to pursue a public-interest career and easily build upon all of the passions that led me to go to law school in the first place.

—N.S., '03;
Harvard Law School

{ 21 }

UNHAPPY LAWYERS
AND HOW TO AVOID
BECOMING ONE

I went looking for stories from people I thought might be role models: successful, happy, together lawyers. Zazi Pope is certainly one, a beautiful, brainy, Harvard Law grad, deputy general counsel of Warner Brothers, Little League mom. One of the questions I asked was whether she'd recommend law school to her children. Her answer surprised me, and reminded me that it was time for chapter and verse on unhappy lawyers . . . and how to avoid becoming one.

I decided to become a lawyer when I was ten. There was a show on TV called Men at Law, *about a bunch of cute cool guys who ran around helping people. I think they added a female character at some point and changed the title to* The Storefront Lawyers. *The characters were really smart, they led exciting lives, and they did good deeds—I was hooked! There was never another career that I seriously considered. I don't regret for one second going to law school, and am thrilled/grateful to have had the opportunity to go to Harvard in particular. Working at a law firm had its ups and downs, but it was a great learning experience and I don't regret any of the time I spent doing that. The only thing I think I do regret is not clerking for a judge—I think that would have been a unique and valuable experience. But I had taken four years off before going to law school (doing human-rights work in South America for much of that time) and I was anxious to "get on with my career."*

I have been at Warner Brothers (supervising litigation) for over ten years, and truly feel as though I have the best lawyer job in the world. The work is intellectually challenging and infinitely varied, I work with smart and fabulous people, and, above all, I get to "have a life"— i.e., spend enough time with my husband and children so that I don't have to live in a state of perpetual guilt. Wow!

Is it sometimes difficult to balance competing demands and interests? Yes. But I'd be a basket case if I only had one or the other. Worst day on the job? Getting hit with a $25 million verdict in the Jenny Jones case. Best day on the job? Getting the judgment reversed by the Michigan Court of Appeals. Typical day: Wake up at six; spend time with Lili, seven, and help get Jeremy, twelve, off to school at six-forty; have breakfast with Lili and Jack [my husband] and get Lili ready for school; seven-forty-five: take her to school and go to work; lunchtime; go to gym (best job perk by far); leave work by six or six-thirty; home before seven; dinner, homework, home maintenance, etc. Eat too much, put kids to bed. Visit with Jack if still awake.

I'm happy. I'm blessed. Exhausted, but blessed.

—ZAZI POPE
Senior Vice President and
Deputy General Counsel,
Warner Brothers

P.S. Notwithstanding the foregoing (as they say in legalese), do I want either one of my children to become lawyers? No!!! I have been incredibly lucky, but I know too many unhappy lawyers out there to want that profession for my children.

ARE LAWYERS REALLY THAT MUCH MORE MISERABLE THAN EVERYBODY ELSE?

Lawyers do tend to be more depressed than other people. If you're a lawyer, you're more likely to drink, get divorced (especially if you're a woman), and see your physical health suffer. You're more likely to commit suicide, and more likely to describe yourself as unhappy. But no one knows for sure whether it's because unhappy people become lawyers or because being lawyers makes them unhappy.

One study of law students (in Arizona) found that while students entered suffering from depression at the same rate as the general population, by the spring of first year, 32 percent said they were suffering from depression, and by the spring of third year, four in ten claimed to be depressed. Two years after graduation, the rate had gone down, but only to 17 percent, which is still double the rate for the general population.

A landmark study in 1990 by Johns Hopkins researchers concluded that lawyers ranked first among all occupational groups for depression, suffering from depression at 3.6 times the rate of nonlawyers who shared the same demographic characteristics. Most groups fall into the 3 percent to 5 percent range for major depression, which is the national average; only lawyers, computer-equipment operators, typists, and kindergarten and special-ed teachers break the 10 percent mark. And who ranks first? Lawyers.

Other statewide studies have found anxiety, hostility, and paranoia in disproportionate numbers among lawyers; lawyers appear to be "prodigious" drinkers, as Professor Patrick Schlitz of Notre Dame Law School describes them, not to mention far more prone to suicide and obsessive-compulsive disorder than the average joe.

At the University of Michigan, which surveys its students regularly, the most recent studies have found declining rates of career satisfaction, especially among lawyers in private practice. One in ten lawyers is eager to get out of the profession. In California, a particularly depressing study by Rand found that as many as half of all lawyers said they wouldn't go to law school again if they had the chance. In North Carolina, almost a quarter of the lawyers in another study said they wouldn't do it again, and 40 percent said they wouldn't encourage their children to be lawyers.

But there is disagreement about the studies, particularly about the implication drawn by some—notably Professor Patrick Schlitz, writing in the *Vanderbilt Law Review*—that big-firm lawyers are most likely to be unhappy. Kathleen Hull, using data from a 1995 survey of Chicago lawyers, argues that big-firm lawyers are neither especially happy nor especially miserable; less likely to be very satisfied, the point Professor Schlitz made, but more likely to be satisfied, and very unlikely to be dissatisfied.

	VERY SATISFIED	SATISFIED	DIS/VD
Large Firm	37%	47%	3%
Public Interest	60%	20%	7%
Government	51%	25%	11%
In-House Counsel	50%	40%	5%
Solo Practitioner	47%	38%	9%

See K. Hull, "Cross-Examining Lawyers' Misery," 52 *Vanderbilt Law Review* 971 (1999); P. Schlitz, "On Being a Happy, Healthy, and Ethical Member of an Unhappy, Unhealthy, and Unethical Profession," 52 *Vanderbilt Law Review* 871 (1999). See also J. Heinz, K. Hull, and A. Harter, "Lawyers and Their Discontents: Findings from a Survey of the Chicago Bar," 74 *Ind. L.J.* 735 (1998–1999).

CAN YOU PREDICT WHO IS LIKELY TO BECOME AN UNHAPPY LAWYER?

I have a theory that most kindergarten teachers can pick out the kids who are likely to get in trouble. Nine times out of ten, they'll be right. I'm beginning to feel the same way about unhappy lawyers. If you get to the point in law school where you're facing the job market and you still don't know what you're doing or why, and you're not doing very well to boot, then I don't need a sociological study to tell me where you're headed.

"Market myself?" The student looked at me like I was crazy. It's rare, but it happens, even at USC. Utterly directionless. He isn't doing on-campus recruiting because his grades are lousy, no activities, no professors or firms or great recommendations, no journals or moot court or anything to make up for it. "What are you going to do?" I ask him.

When I finished clerking, I was trying to decide whether to go to work as the special assistant to the chief counsel of the Senate Judiciary Committee or whether to go to a law firm. Of course the law-firm job paid twice as much. Of course I had no money, never had.

Stephen Breyer, who was about to take the job as chief counsel, and his predecessor, David Boies, who was finishing it up, came over to see me at the Supreme Court, where I was clerking for Justice Stevens. We all sat down in the quiet chambers. They commented that it was absolutely nothing like the Senate Judiciary Committee. They suggested that I come spend a day shadowing them. Steve was already shadowing

David, getting ready for their transition. I might as well shadow Steve shadowing David.

I had already worked in two law firms. Many people thrive in law firms. I tended to forget to fill out billing sheets. My favorite projects would be pro bono. But I am not immune to pack mentality, the pull of loans, or the belief that the perfect high-paying job still lurks around the next corner. So I'd gone back on the firm-interview circuit again, with all the other law clerks, since I happened to have the most loans. Still, law firms were so quiet.

I went to shadow the guys. We had meeting after meeting. Different groups of (very) young lawyers came in, sometimes with lobbyists in tow, to discuss whatever: like the antitrust exemption for Major League Baseball (the commissioner and the chief counsel of baseball were working me, "as well they should," someone pointed out, "who else was going to end up writing the memo . . . ?"), and then the crime bill, and the ACLU people were screaming bloody murder, and then there was trucking deregulation, which the trucking industry wasn't so sure about.

I signed on that day. It took me about a minute to remember who I was. And then Senator Kennedy, within months of my arrival, announced his candidacy for president, and I ended up in the campaign, and as the campaign did less and less well, the people with big mortgages and bigger jobs departed, and by the summer of 1980, there I was again, sitting across the table from the top aides of the president of the United States, negotiating on what the platform fights would be at the convention, and traveling around the country with Senator Kennedy and Ron Brown, who later became chairman of the Democratic Party and secretary of commerce, before dying in a plane crash over Bosnia.

I ran the platform for Senator Kennedy. We put reproductive freedom and sexual orientation in the Democratic platform for the first time. It was a really big deal. These were considered "dangerous" issues at the time. I was taking on the president of the United States, working with Bella Abzug, Eleanor Smeal, Gloria Steinem, Norman Lear, the early leaders of the gay-rights movement in America, many of whom are now dead of AIDS. I was the only woman in a room of ten men negotiating the deals for the New York convention.

I ran the boiler room in Madison Square Garden. We were fighting for the heart and soul of the Democratic Party, or so it seemed at the time. The room was full of phones connected to the floor, meant to provide instantaneous communications to our delegate whips. Kennedy was due to speak later in the evening. We were jazzed. At the time Atlanta Mayor Andy Young was speaking *against* one of our planks. Did I know he had cleared his speech with my boss, eager not to offend? I didn't, and no one who did, or outranked me, was in the room. I was hanging out with Rick Stearns, who had been a McGovern delegate hunter and went on to be a prosecutor and is now a federal judge. We decided to do a dry run: How long would it take between the time I gave the sign, and all Kennedy delegates (one third of the total on the floor) were on their feet yelling "no, no, no"? The signal was to follow Pennsylvania, where my mentor, the late, great Paul Tully, a graduate of Penn Law School, who was one of the great political organizers of all time, was running things. Time would be measured according to when the anchors broke into Young's speech. The room hushed. I gave the order. The desk people picked up the phones. We turned up the TVs. The chants moved like a roar across the floor. Andy Young's face turned green. All the anchors broke in. The delegates were on their feet. Ninety seconds. "Down," I yelled. They picked up the phones. It stopped as fast as it started. Andy Young went back to his speech. The anchors went back to their notes. I looked at Rick Stearns. Too slow, we decided. We did it again.

"The Kennedy people have control of this convention," the anchors all announced. Sixty-eight seconds. Not bad for a girl from Lynn. I was twenty-seven at the time. Who needs money?

{ 22 }

WORK THAT MATTERS; PROFESSIONALISM; DEFINING IT FOR YOURSELF

*"Never forget that your reputation for integrity
is your most important asset."*

—JUSTICE JOHN PAUL STEVENS
U.S. SUPREME COURT

Most law schools produce civil lawyers in part because they are the people who come to campus offering jobs and they are the people who are willing to pay the most for your services. It is a measure of both the market and inertia that so many students become civil lawyers.

**The easiest thing to do if you're
not sure what you want to do:
Put everything off a year.**

Summary of Requirements for Admission to Practice Law in California

To be admitted to practice law in California, an applicant must:

- Complete the necessary general education.
- Register with the Committee of Bar Examiners as a law student or attorney applicant.
- Complete the requisite legal education.
- File an application to take the First-Year Law Students' Examination and pass, or establish exemption from the examination (accomplished by attending an ABA-approved law school).
- File an application for a moral-character determination and receive a positive moral-character determination from the Committee of Bar Examiners.
- File an application to take the bar examination and, after eligibility has been confirmed, take and pass the examination.
- Apply for and pass the Multistate Professional Responsibility Examination with a scaled score of 79.00 or greater.
- Be in compliance with California court-ordered child- or family-support obligations.

Source: Bar Exam/Admisssions, The State Bar of California, <http://www.calbar.ca.gov/state/calbar/calbar_generic.jsp?sCategoryPath=/Home/Attorney%20Resources/Bar%20Exam>. © 2004 by the State Bar of California.

WHY YOU SHOULD CLERK

- The absolute best job you can possibly get coming out of law school is a judicial clerkship.
- Because so many law students don't realize this, it is easier than it should be to get one.
- It can automatically bounce you up the food chain a notch or two, if not more.
- A recommendation from a judge makes your next job much easier to get.

Say "clerkships" and immediately everyone thinks about the federal court and the top 10 percent. Yes, that's part of the picture. If you're holding a handful of aces, or at least a lot of high cards, I would absolutely recommend that you apply for a clerkship.

Yes, you will make less money than you would have by going straight to a firm. And if you choose wrong, or are wrongly chosen, there's no escape: the one great danger of a clerkship is that if you end up with someone miserably unpleasant to work for, there's no transferring to another partner. You're stuck.

But the upside potential is enormous. For one thing, you get a view of the law the likes of which you would otherwise have to wait twenty, thirty years for—or never get at all. The people whose briefcases you may be carrying for the next decade or so will treat you like a king or queen. You'll get to see a range of different firms in action, and you may be surprised by what you see. You get to put off making decisions about what to do with the rest of your life (or at least the next few years) until you've had a chance to catch your breath. You put yourself in a position to get a much better job than you might otherwise have, particularly if you do a good job as a clerk, and your judge is willing to pick up the phone and start making calls for you.

And best of all: if, like me, you're lucky enough to clerk for an extraordinary judge or two, you get an amazing experience out of it. It is the nature of the beast that judges can't talk to the world about their cases: they're stuck, by the rules of confidentiality, talking to their clerks. And so they do. And so you learn.

You can minimize the risk of getting stuck with a demon by asking around. Let's face it: there are no secrets. The demons are well known. You apply to them at your own risk. Since the rule of thumb is that you can't turn a judge down, you never apply for a clerkship you don't want. The difficult ones are legendary. Should you believe what you hear? In this realm, yes. Should you do it anyway? Sometimes. It depends on the trade-off, your temperament, what you can handle. There was a legendary judge, who shall remain nameless, who had a legendary temper; some people could take it, some didn't. You knew it. People used to ask if you had a difficult grandfather.

CLERKSHIPS AREN'T ONLY FOR STRAIGHT-A STUDENTS FROM THE T14 LAW SCHOOLS.

Think like a Realtor, only this time, in reverse. Everyone wants to clerk in Boston, New York, and Washington; so think Newark. Everyone wants Los Angeles, San Francisco, and San Diego; so think Sacramento, and Carson City, Nevada.

Think state courts as well as federal courts. Think about all the places that might not be your first choices, geographically or judicially speaking, and you don't need four aces to win. Think about being a court clerk, or a pro se clerk, rather than clerking for an individual judge. Keep up with who has just been confirmed by the U.S. Senate Judiciary Committee, and who has just been appointed by the governor of your state.

WHAT ARE THE KEYS TO GETTING A CLERKSHIP?

Grades, recommendations, and making a personal connection. Your grades are what they are. Your connections? I never had them. If you do, congratulations. Recommendations? Remember that professor I told you to compliment or, better yet, work for? This is one reason why.

Creativity also comes into play. Beyond location, think about matches. Did you play football? Find a judge who did. Better yet, some esoteric sport, hobby, hometown, alma mater, common tie, interest, religious background, anything that will help forge a connection. Find something that you and he have in common. The more unique the better.

In many chambers, current clerks do the screening—so you need to work them. Many judges rely on past clerks for recommendations, so you need to find them. Does it sound like a campaign? It is.

DOES DEBT DETERMINE WHO DOES WHAT?

The answer may surprise you. In an important article in the *New York University Law Review,* Professor, now Dean, Richard Revesz and Professor Lewis Kornhauser used extensive empirical data to prove that: "contrary to commonly held beliefs, law school debt does not have a significant effect on attorneys' first job choice."

What does, then? "Career plans to enter the not-for-profit sector make it significantly more likely that a graduate will take a job in that sector."

Students come in with their passions, and if they are lucky, graduate with them. It's not how much they borrow, but who they are, that counts. Not so surprising, is it?

Race and gender matter in career plans, and therefore in career choice. So does the vast gap in pay between the for-profit and the not-for-profit sector. Indeed, the most stunning aspect of the article are the numbers on the gap.

In 1980, entry-level salaries in elite law firms in Chicago, Los Angeles, and Washington, D.C., were 39.2 percent, 45.6 percent, and 56.9 percent higher than the entry-level salary in the federal government, according to Kornhauser and Revesz. By 1990, these private salaries were respectively 134.2 percent, 142 percent, and 136.4 percent higher; nonelite firm salaries were 60.6 percent, 70.6 percent, and 53.9 percent higher . . .

ENTRY-LEVEL SALARIES IN CURRENT DOLLARS FOR THREE PRACTICE SETTINGS			
YEAR	N.Y. NONELITE	N.Y. ELITE	FEDERAL GOVERNMENT
1978	$23,000	$27,500	$18,258
1979	$21,000	$29,842	$19,263
1980	$22,500	$34,891	$20,611
1981	$24,000	$40,042	$22,486
1982	$25,000	$41,700	$23,566
1983	$26,500	$43,300	$24,508
1984	$36,000	$47,203	$25,366
1985	$39,000	$49,217	$26,381
1986	$40,000	$63,500	$26,381
1987	$46,000	$65,600	$27,172

ENTRY-LEVEL SALARIES IN CURRENT DOLLARS FOR THREE PRACTICE SETTINGS

YEAR	N.Y. NONELITE	N.Y. ELITE	FEDERAL GOVERNMENT
1988	$49,000	$72,842	N/A
1989	$57,000	$79,245	$28,852
1990	$59,500	$82,217	$29,891
1991	$60,000	$81,878	$31,116
1992	N/A	$81,980	$32,423
1993	N/A	$81,870	$33,623

ENTRY-LEVEL SALARIES IN CONSTANT 1990 DOLLARS FOR THREE PRACTICE SETTINGS

YEAR	N.Y. NONELITE	N.Y. ELITE	FEDERAL GOVERNMENT
1978	$46,000	$55,000	$36,516
1979	$37,821	$53,745	$34,692
1980	$35,685	$55,337	$32,689
1981	$34,392	$57,380	$32,222
1982	$33,775	$56,337	$31,838
1983	$34,688	$56,680	$32,081
1984	$45,180	$59,240	$31,834
1985	$47,229	$59,602	$31,947
1986	$47,680	$75,692	$31,446
1987	$52,854	$75,374	$31,221
1988	$54,096	$80,418	$30,598
1989	$60,078	$83,524	$30,410
1990	$59,500	$82,217	$29,891
1991	$57,480	$78,439	$29,809
1992	N/A	$76,228	$30,186
1993	N/A	$73,847	$30,362

Source: Lewis A. Kornhauser & Richard L. Revesz, "Legal Education and Entry into the Legal Profession: The Role of Race, Gender, and Educational Debt," *NYU Law Review* 829, (1995), 867–68.

HOW DO YOU GET TO BE A TV LAWYER?

I have the "weirdest" lawyer job. I am the "accidental anchor." I went to law school to become an old-fashioned trial lawyer (like the lawyers in my hometown of Appleton, Wisconsin). I had no intention of ever being on TV. It never crossed my mind. There was no such thing as a "TV legal analyst" when I grew up or when I got out of law school in 1979. Perry Mason was the only "lawyer" on TV, and frankly, his life as a trial lawyer looked pretty damn good to me. That's what I wanted to be: a trial lawyer.

When I graduated from law school I did hang up a shingle and practice law for about fifteen years. I tried everything from small claims to first-degree murder and argued in many courts of appeal. My boutique law firm took anything that walked in the door (we could not afford to be fussy). Then one day I agreed to do a "three-day gig" on CNN to comment on the William Kennedy Smith trial (CNN's first trial on TV) and I just never left TV.

My biggest thrill has always been the honor of representing someone in court. It is also the hardest thing I have ever done. The responsibility of being a trial lawyer is immense and the intellectual challenge is enormous. It is also very physically demanding—round-the-clock work and never-ending worry. Being a trial lawyer is not for the weak or the lazy. It is for those with great passion for justice and a desire to win.

Today I have a different responsibility and I have the thrill of having the "best seat" on every major legal issue (and, of course, other topics as well). I love this job. I meet everyone and people from all walks of life. I would hate it if someone insisted I pick between being a trial lawyer or an anchor with real legal experience.

If the question is "Would I go to law school all over again?," the answer is an unequivocal yes. You can't get better training for whatever career you pursue—including journalism. Legal education teaches you how to

ask questions, how to investigate facts, how facts are different from opin-
ions, how to verify and corroborate, the importance of fairness and justice,
etc. This is extremely important in all occupations. Plus, if you go into
journalism, you get the pleasure of saying "unlike journalists who simply
declare themselves journalists, I took an exam of competency (the bar!)."
—GRETA VAN SUSTEREN,
Host, On the Record,
Fox News Channel

I love hearing stories like the one my friend Greta van Susteren tells in her recent book, *My Turn at the Bully Pulpit,* about
one of the most mocked lawsuits of recent times, that against
McDonald's for serving scalding coffee that burned a woman;
was actually grounded in a corporate decision to heat the coffee
to a temperature where they knew that, if spilled, it would cause
serious burns; McDonald's, in fact, served its coffee substantially
hotter than its competitors; they did so believing that the coffee
would be brought home or to the office and consumed there;
when it spilled and severely burned the particular woman, caus-
ing extensive medical injuries, they refused her reasonable re-
quests simply to compensate her for medical expenses and lost
wages; only then did she resort to litigation to force them to reduce the temperature of the coffee so that others wouldn't be
burned. Doesn't sound so silly after all, does it?

Erwin Chemerinsky was my colleague for the last fifteen years.
He has just left USC for Duke, and they are very lucky indeed
to have him:

The hardest part of being a lawyer is losing. Obviously, the more one
cares, the harder it is to lose. This year, I argued and lost a case, 5–4, in

the United States Supreme Court, Lockyer *v.* Andrade. *My client, Leandro Andrade, received a life sentence, with no possibility of parole for fifty years, for stealing $153 worth of children's videotapes from Kmart stores.*

Andrade had no violent prior offenses. He committed three burglaries in 1983 and served two and a half years in prison for these offenses. In 1995, he went into a Kmart store and stole five children's videotapes, including Cinderella *and* Snow White, *worth about $80. He was seen on an overhead camera and he was stopped at the store's exit, where the videotapes were confiscated and he was arrested. Less than a week later, he went into another Kmart and stole four children's videotapes, including* Free Willy 2 *and* Batman Forever, *worth about $70. Again, he was caught because of the video-surveillance cameras, the tapes were confiscated, and he was arrested.*

This usually would be regarded as the crime of "petty theft," stealing less than $400 of merchandise, in California. However, if a person committing petty theft has a prior property conviction, then the individual can be charged with the felony crime, "petty theft with a prior." Ironically, if Andrade's prior crimes had been rape and murder, his maximum sentence would have been one year in jail; "petty theft with a prior" requires that the previous conviction be for a property offense. In California, two counts of petty theft with a prior are punishable by three years and eight months in prison. But Andrade was sentenced under California's three-strikes law. Although twenty-six states have three-strikes laws, California's is unique in that the third strike need not be a serious or violent felony. Any felony is a basis for applying the law and Andrade's petty theft with a prior was used to impose a life sentence; since he had stolen videotapes twice, his sentence was life in prison, with no possibility of parole for fifty years. In no other state in the country could Andrade have received this sentence. As Justice Stephen Breyer observed in dissent in a companion case, prior to California's three-strikes law, no person in the history of the United States had re-

ceived a life sentence for shoplifting. In fact, at the time Andrade was sentenced to life in prison for stealing the videotapes, the maximum sentence for rape in California was eight years in prison, for manslaughter it was eleven years, and for second-degree murder it was fifteen years. After Andrade's sentence was upheld in the California courts, he filed a habeas corpus petition in federal court. Federal courts can provide relief to state prisoners if there has been a constitutional violation. Andrade filed his habeas corpus petition without an attorney's help. The government does not have to provide a lawyer to criminal defendants filing habeas corpus petitions. The federal trial court dismissed the petition without an opinion. Andrade filed an appeal in the United States Court of Appeals for the Ninth Circuit. In the fall of 2000, the court appointed me to represent him.

My argument seemed strong. For at least a century, the Supreme Court has held that a sentence which is grossly disproportionate to the crime constitutes cruel and unusual punishment in violation of the Eighth Amendment. If anything is grossly disproportionate, it is a life sentence, with no possibility of parole for fifty years, for shoplifting.

Andrade's story was particularly compelling. He was an army veteran and a father of three; he developed a drug problem while in the military. He never had committed any violent crime. As I wrote the briefs in Andrade's case, I was bewildered by why a prosecutor would seek a life sentence for shoplifting, why a judge would impose such a sentence, and why the state attorney general would fight so hard to uphold it. There is nothing in Andrade's record that warranted such a draconian punishment. I argued his case in the court of appeals in San Francisco in May 2001 and I was thrilled six months later when the court ruled in Andrade's favor. In a long and careful opinion, the court explained why Andrade's sentence was cruel and unusual punishment.

Andrade's victory offered hope to 360 other people who were serving life sentences in California for "petty theft with a prior." In fact, I was deluged with letters from prisoners and their families expressing optimism that their life sentences for minor offenses might be reduced. The Ninth Circuit appointed me to represent two other individuals, Richard Napoleon Brown and Ernest Bray, who were sentenced to life in prison with no possibility of parole for twenty-five years for "petty theft with a prior" for stealing, respectively, a $25 car alarm and three videotapes. I argued their cases before the court on December 12, 2001, and the Ninth Circuit ruled in their favor in February 2002.

Unfortunately, California Attorney General Bill Lockyer sought to have the Supreme Court review the Ninth Circuit's decisions. Nothing in California law required him to do so. On April 1, 2002, the Supreme Court granted review in Lockyer v. Andrade. I spent much of the next few months working on my brief to the Supreme Court.

On November 5, 2002, I stood before the justices to argue Andrade's case. I had done everything I could think of to prepare. I had participated in three moot courts, where lawyers peppered me with questions to help me anticipate what the justices were likely to ask. I had spent countless hours rereading the cases and the briefs and planning responses to questions. As I argued on Andrade's behalf, I was very consciously aware of what was at stake: if I won, Leandro Andrade was sure to be a free man within weeks of the decision; but if I lost, he would spend the rest of his life in prison for shoplifting. If I won, 360 others serving life sentences for shoplifting likely would be released; if I lost, there would be little to give them hope. If Andrade's sentence was not grossly disproportionate, it is hard to imagine the sentence which would violate the Eighth Amendment. After the argument was over, I felt that I would have tremendously enjoyed the experience if not for the weight of how much was at stake. The Supreme Court does not inform anyone of when a particular decision is going to be announced. However, it is possible to find out the days on which there will be decisions; there's just no way to know which cases will be handed down. A friend, David Pike, who covers the Supreme Court *for the* Daily Journal, *kindly offered to call me as soon as the Court announced the ruling in* Andrade. *My guess, and it was just a guess based on the Court's calendar, was that the ruling would come down when it was in session on February 25, February 26, March 4, or March 5. On each of the nights before those days, I found it hard to sleep. That's unusual for me; little usually interferes with my sleeping. I slept fine the night before the Supreme Court argument. But the anticipation of the decision and what it would mean was hard to bear. The Court announces its decisions at ten A.M., eastern time, at the start of its sessions. At seven o'clock pacific time on those days, I anxiously waited for the phone to ring. I figured if I didn't hear anything by seven-fifteen it meant no decision; it usually takes the Court about fifteen minutes to announce its rulings. On February 25, February 26, and March 4 no phone call came. March 5 was the Court's last day in session for almost a month. If the decision wasn't announced that day, there would be no ruling for several more weeks. At seven, as I was getting my younger children ready for school, I listened for the phone. By seven-twenty-five, when it was time to take my eight-year-old son to catch the school bus, I was convinced that the decision had not come that day. Just to be sure, I listened carefully to the headlines on the seven-thirty news on the radio, and when no mention was made of Supreme Court decisions, I relaxed and walked my son from the car to the bus stop. Just as my son was boarding the bus, the cell phone in my pocket rang. David Pike immediately said, "Bad news, you lost five–four. O'Connor wrote the opinion." We spoke for a few more minutes. As I drove to my office, I felt numb. I called my wife to tell her of the decision and then called my oldest son, who was in college in Colorado, to inform him. Both, along with my other two sons, had been at the Supreme Court in November.*

By the time I got to my office, the sense of loss began to hit me. I immediately accessed and printed the decision. As I read it, I felt out-

rage that a majority of the Court saw no problem with imposing a life sentence for shoplifting and profound sadness for what the decision meant for Andrade and others in his situation. There were dozens and dozens of media calls. The first came from a friend who works at a local-news radio station. I literally was in tears as I tried to do the interview. I tried unsuccessfully to call Andrade in prison and then to reach the family members of my clients. The mother of one of my clients, a man who received a life sentence for stealing a $128 television set, asked what they could do next. I was at a loss to think of anything. Over the days that followed, I had the constant feeling of sadness and loss not unlike when someone close dies. I still feel quite devastated by the decision. If one justice in the majority had voted differently, Leandro Andrade would be a free man today. He already has served seven years for stealing those videotapes. Now he must go forty-three more years before he even is eligible for parole at the age of eighty-six.

Losing sucks especially when the consequences are so large.

I don't think losing is nearly as bad as never engaging in the fight at all. A law degree is a license to do work that matters, but it's hardly a guarantee. Too many lawyers get stuck filing useless lawsuits or defending them, not so much because they want to as because they can't figure out what else to do. Dreary doesn't begin to describe it. Scumbag lawyers don't grow up that way. They become that for want of the creativity to become something better. Don't do it. Remember the rule. Expand your view. Look at opposites.

I have a student thriving on the police department: she'll either become a prosecutor one of these days, or she'll be the chief. Need I add that the DA's office wouldn't hire her straight out?

I know lawyers running charter schools. I know lawyers teaching school. Don't be limited to lawyers' jobs. Use a law degree for all it's worth. Demand more, knowing that you will need that.

The irony is that these so-called third-tier schools worry desperately about their students passing the bar as if there are good lawyer jobs waiting for their graduates when just the opposite may be true; they owe their students far more precisely because there aren't.

Ask any lawyer who has gone into business whether his law degree has helped him and the answer will be, absolutely, yes. When Harvard Law School gathered its richest alums to begin its first capital campaign in the early 1980s, it discovered that virtually none of them were lawyers; the largest single category was real-estate developers. Were they glad they'd gone to law school? Absolutely. Were they grateful? Very much so. Were they happy to be doing what they were doing, hiring lawyers instead of being them? Sure thing.

I once said to one of my students who had spent years defending stupid insurance claims (the best job he could get, he would tell me, which was true only in the narrowest sense): "You know, if you had put this much energy into working for the insurance company, you'd probably be running it by now." He seriously agreed. He said he was smarter than any of the executives he'd ever dealt with. It was, however, the first time he'd ever thought of it, which was what I found stunning. That's how trapped he was.

So why do we keep telling students that they have to be lawyers? None of us are. Why don't we free them, at some point, to take over the insurance company? Why don't we see a law degree as a license to run the world, so long as you live by the rule of law when you do . . .

I was walking home the other night and I ran into one of my former students. She is, she happily told me, a working screenwriter. Couldn't be having a better time. Her law school boyfriend, now husband, is president of production for a television network. Loves his work. Neither of them is a lawyer. She laughed. "Much better," she said. "But you were our favorite professor," she quickly added, lest I be insulted. How did they get these great jobs? They were entertainment lawyers. They got to know executives. They never would have gotten where they are if they hadn't been lawyers. Of course, they hated being lawyers, she explained. But it all worked out. She got in her Porsche. We smiled. "Nice suit," I said. Looked like a thousand bucks to me. I don't own such nice suits. She looked great. I never would have recognized her from law school.

> If you can't get a good-enough job as a civil lawyer to make it satisfying, find a specialty that is considered less prestigious (but may be more lucrative, or more rewarding). Or go be a government lawyer. Or don't be a lawyer at all. But don't do work you need to apologize for. Or work you hate. You didn't struggle to get into law school, and work hard for three years, to hate your work . . .

There isn't a city in America that doesn't need good, honest lawyers who will do family law, divorce law, and criminal defense work. Be one. Go work in the city attorney's office, where fancy-shmancy grads almost never set foot; ditto for the children's courts; check out city and state government;

the Justice Department Honors Program; take the Foreign Service exam. Go use your legal skills working in a country no one else wants to work in. Try to figure out what it is that makes the rule of law work. Look at what's going on in Iraq, I say.

You think con law is challenging, try writing a constitution. The amazing part of venturing off the beaten path is seeing what people do with law degrees when you get there, and the rewards they reap. If I were twenty-five today, I'd be trying to figure out how you create constitutional models in countries that have never had a fair legal system. I'd be off to China and the Middle East and the former Soviet Union.

Don't think of your town or even your state as the stage; think of the world. Don't say law is boring. It's anything but. Some people who practice it are, and so are some practices. But until you start making big money, you don't start needing it. You have a kind of freedom before you take your first high-paying job that you will never have again once you do. It is impossible for most of us, particularly those of us who have had so little for so long, to resist the desire to have something. That's how you end up in silver handcuffs. If you're not in them yet, use that freedom ("just another word for nothing left to lose," after all) to push yourself further, not to fall apart. Why don't you go abroad? I asked one of my directionless students, after I'd been expounding on the challenges of reinventing the rule of law in places like Yugoslavia. He could barely make his way to the Valley, and I wanted him to consider the former Yugoslavia. Why not?

If you find yourself miserable as a lawyer, be glad you're not a doctor (since no one ever understands why doctors leave medical jobs) and have the guts to leave, and put your legal training to better use. If you don't want to be a lawyer, don't. Use your legal training for something else.

There are great jobs—as developers, builders, around the world. Running and building charter schools. As teachers and principals. Managing racetracks. Running newspapers. Running news divisions. As a reporter. As a television producer. Owning restaurants. Owning sports teams. Running sports teams. Being a cop. Running a police department. Covering a police department. Writing novels about police departments. Writing TV shows about police departments. Making movies about police departments. Suing police departments. Defending police departments. Running hospitals. Running for office. Running campaigns. Running countries. Running casinos. Running insurance companies. Selling stock. Creating stock markets. Creating constitutions.

It's not my job to make the list.

"But I've got loans," the student said. I know. Or silver handcuffs. Or tuitions to pay. Or a mortgage.

More places than you think have various loan-repayment plans that allow students to defer, or reduce, loan repayments depending upon what they do or what salary they receive. Some law schools have them, and more are under pressure to start them. There's a federal law authorizing federal agencies to offer loan repayment as an inducement to recruitment, although, in the current budget crunch, few have taken advantage of the authorization to do so.

In some jobs, you can also negotiate your own loan-repayment plan, as I did with Harvard, when I was working in politics and not getting paid. I know exactly what the payments on $100,000 of debt are. The bottom line is that you don't have to do work you hate to make them. Can you sell? Manage? Teach? Run things? What do you like to do? You still have to work.

"I hate practicing law . . . I don't think I should be doing this anymore . . . I wish I could stop . . . I'm counting the years . . . I'm beginning to wonder whether there is any alternative for me . . . At least I get to take good vacations and get good hobbies." I cannot even begin to tell you how often I get calls from people who are unhappy practicing law. Maybe I shouldn't be doing this, they say. So try something else, say I. See if it's you or your career. I make suggestions. I tell you what happens most of the time. Nothing. They want to keep making six or seven figures or whatever. Up to you.

"Regarding law and my career," Dean Christopher Edley of Boalt writes, "help has come from examples rather than advice. One example was a friend, George, about twenty years my senior, who was a litigator specializing in environmental law at a major D.C. law firm. He told me that the only thing he liked about his work was that it gave him the flexibility and the income to take fabulous vacations and have exciting hobbies. I realized that I would never make his choice. For me, the job must in itself provide a day-to-day sense of satisfaction and, indeed, fulfillment. I've been extraordinarily fortunate to be able to meet that standard."

I'm with my old friend Chris: good vacations and good hobbies are not reason for a life lived, a mind spent, a soul used.

When I think back on the day Steve Breyer and David Boies came to recruit me at the Supreme Court, I think of them both being old, and of course, they were both very young, as I see it now, twenty-five years later, looking at where they were in their careers, one a young professor at Harvard, the other a young partner at Cravath.

And they had both taken leaves from their jobs to make much less money and share an office with who knows how many people as chief counsel of the Senate Judiciary Committee, which is certainly a great job by most standards except those of Harvard professors or Cravath partners, most of whom thought both of them crazy.

"A staff job," somebody said to me, when I said I was going to work for Steve on the Judiciary Committee. "Not even a deputy attorney general . . ." There is no snob like a Harvard snob. As for Cravath, how many partners leave to do anything, other than die?

So there they were, these two upstarts, and today one of them is on the Supreme Court of the United States and the other, best as I can tell, is not only himself the founder of the only new entrant into the most prestigious law firms in America but is widely considered to be the top trial lawyer in the country.

Those two guys. Is it just a coincidence that they came to recruit me twenty-five years ago?

Of course not. They had guts. And drive. They dared to leave the beaten path. Steve Breyer wouldn't have been confirmed for the First Circuit if he hadn't developed a relationship with Strom Thurmond while working as chief counsel, and he certainly wouldn't have been appointed to the Supreme Court had it not been for his relationship with Ted Kennedy.

WHICH WILL YOU BE: A DOER OR A WHINER?

If you free yourself from the constraints of saying, I'm on this escalator with everyone else, to Firm Number One, and ask the more fundamental question, what do YOU want to do with your law degree, your legal training, your talent, half of your life?

Ultimately, *the reason that there are so many miserable lawyers is that they don't do anything about it.* It's not that they couldn't find other jobs. They could. Most of them don't even need the money, or they don't need it half as much as they need their souls (although they think they do). So why don't they do something?

Most corporate lawyers I know would be much happier if they took a break to do any of the following: Be prosecutors. Work in Liberia. Design and advise military tribunals. Overhaul small-claims court. Serve as senior counsel to a Senate Committee.

So why don't they do it? Can't Afford it. Afraid to go looking. No one asked me. If someone asked . . .

Don't ask me, ask them. Ask yourself. Look in the mirror.

How do you start? By starting. Look around. Look at everybody you know who has a law degree, including all the people who are doing things that have nothing to do with law. What job or jobs would you like to have now, or in five years?

Who would you like to be? Make a list of every person you or anyone you know knows who could possibly help you get there. Not necessarily today, but sometime. Now figure out how to approach them, and get them to sit down with you and agree to help you. The only way to really get a job that's not an escalator stop is to get people to help you get it. You do not get the job you want by résumé campaigns based in the phone book; you get the job that wants you that way.

Make a better résumé. Write to people you want to meet first to introduce yourself. Write a careful, smart, intelligent letter, asking for their help. Tell them who you are, what you are trying/hoping to do, looking for, why you are writing to them, what you are hoping they can do—spend time, give you leads, etc. . . .

What will impress these people is your passion: the research you've done, the commitment you demonstrate, that you care about something, know what you want to do, where you want to go, who you are, what kind of contribution you want to make, that you have a soul and a plan and the wherewithal and the education and the guts and the determination to get there.

You know about the Conventional Stuff. Using what you have.

USE THE CAREER-SERVICES OFFICE.

Most people don't. Get everything you can from them. Ask for help. A lot of it. You'll only get what you ask for. The more specific you are, the better. Say, "I'm looking for . . ." and then tell them what you're interested in, what kind of alums you'd like to talk to, who has jobs now like the ones you'd like to have. Remember—the key to finding a job is finding people in that world who will ultimately think of you when they hear of something—so you want to be out there, as a real person, who is well regarded . . .

USE THE FACULTY.

If you have a professor(s) on your side, use them. Go see them. Ask for help. Letters. Leads. Contacts.

USE WHOM YOU HAVE.

What if you didn't get an offer from your firm last summer. See what they're willing to say about it . . . Is there an agreed-upon "code." That it wasn't the right fit? Is there a lawyer there who will give you a positive recommendation? Can you work out an appropriate saving-grace story, like the right fit, "we concluded together that it wasn't a good match . . ."? If you don't get a summer job, consider volunteering part-time, and using it as an opportunity to pick up a reference: be absolutely crass about what you need in exchange for volunteering—an opportunity to work for someone who will mentor you through the job process; whoever the right fit for *that* would be, and be clear about just what you're looking for.

Do not apologize for using people: all it gets you is entry in the door. No one gets you a job. All they do is get you an opportunity to get yourself the job. Let's be clear about that. You get yourself the job. Or lose it. So say thank you, but if someone in your mother's beauty parlor knows someone, those of us who are not to privilege bred need not say sorry.

My mother was in the beauty parlor one day in 1981—Raffaele's (Ralph's) in Swampscott—when she told everyone that I was thinking of teaching part-time at Penn Law School. I'd never even considered teaching when I left Harvard, but Reagan had just been elected, the plans I'd made with Ron Brown to take over the Senate Judiciary Committee (he was going to be chief counsel, I would be general counsel—at twenty-eight) had gone up in smoke when the Democrats lost the Senate. So why not take the train up to Penn one day a week to teach? Out of the blue, I'd gotten this call to teach a course in Women and the Law. What did everyone think? my mother asked.

Carla Herwitz was not pleased. A partner in a Boston firm herself, a rarity in those days; her husband was a Harvard law professor. She took the news directly from Ralph's to Dave, who took it to Al Sacks, then the dean, who called me in Washington the next day. I had only told one person about the Penn offer. My mother. How did you know? I asked Al Sacks. Actually, he said, Dave Herwitz brought it to my attention; apparently Carla learned of this. Ralph's, I thought. That's how I got to Harvard. Via Ralph's. He still does my hair when I visit my mother.

Everybody worries about graduating from law school ready to pass the bar. There's something almost funny about it, in the sense that the first thing everyone then does is sign up for the bar course, properly so, given the stakes; and the bar course teaches you, all over again, down to the word, everything you need to know for the bar, and all you have to do is pass the bar.

On the other hand, I can't tell you how many students get to within seconds of graduation with absolutely no clue as to what aspect of legal practice, thinking, policy, anything in the world, interests them. Nothing. Professionally agnostic, or maybe that's just what they think they're supposed to be with me, in which case it's simply a sign of how badly you can read someone (watch out on such misreadings). But I don't think so. When I ask them what was their favorite course, clinic, externship, anything—nothing.

If you don't come into law school with passions, use your time to develop them. If you have them, use the job search to let them explode, and see where they take you.

If this all sounds familiar, it should. The job search, after all, is the last chance to answer the question about what you were doing applying to law school in the first place. It really is the final exam. You need an answer, by the end, or you'll end up, by default, in someone else's life. The answer is the job you take, or create, the work you do, what it is, and how you do it. If it isn't enough for you, you end up miserable. The answer to the paradox. The failure to get out is the simple function of getting paid too much to walk away without some sacrifice. We sell our souls too cheap. Former students come to me all the time. "I'm unhappy," they say.

The further off the beaten track you go, the more it's up to you to find it.

Twenty-five years ago, Jim Flug worked on the Senate Judiciary Committee for Ted Kennedy. He's a brilliant guy. He was one of the stars on the Hill. He did energy issues. Then he went into private practice and made money. He always told himself that at sixty, when he'd made enough money, educated his kids, he'd return to public service. He turned sixty, and he started looking around. He almost took a job on the 9/11 Commission but then Teddy called him and told him the chief counsel's job on Judiciary was open. How could he not take it?

He called right after Arnold got elected. He had this idea about how maybe he could retroactively blue-slip (veto) a judicial nominee . . . Vintage Flugian. What the heck? I thought. I'll pass it along. Anyway, it was good to talk to him again. That's my life.

Go create yours. I think of law as the civic religion that holds us together. So make it a blessing.

INDEX